Fully
Familiar
Phrases

Fairly Familiar Phrases

A reference book for court reporters, notereaders-transcribers, scopists, secretaries, and anyone who is interested in words.

By Mary Louise Gilman

Copyright 1984, National Court Reporters Association
ISBN 1-881859-03-7

PREFACE

Back in the spring and summer of 1982, the *National Shorthand Reporter* ran a series called "Fairly Familiar Phrases." It went over well, and some readers cried "More!" That sparked this considerably expanded version.

We might ask two questions prompted by the title. First, what is a phrase? I used the criterion that it must contain two or more words—but the two words could be hyphenated. (You might argue that some entries are really hyphenated words, not phrases.) Speaking of hyphens, I found great divergence among dictionaries on hyphenating. I settled on Webster's *Ninth New Collegiate Dictionary* as my authority. (That meant I had to throw out "mealy-mouthed," which appeared in the original list, because the *Ninth* gives it as one word. As William Safire wrote in the *New York Times* a few months ago, its hyphen simply wore out. Because of its interesting origin, I parted with the word reluctantly.)

Next, what is "fairly familiar"? If you've done much reading—and listening—you've probably run across most of the entries here. They would give you no problem in context. But, like me, you wouldn't be able to define them all "cold." And what's familiar to me may not be to you, and vice versa.

I rejected as *too* familiar such common phrases as "once in a while" and "now and then"—though, on examination, they're rather interesting and might well puzzle the foreigner struggling to learn English. Clichés like "at this point in time," "ballpark figure," and "bottom line," which we hear in court and elsewhere ad nauseam, got short shrift. (You *will* find "ad nauseam" and "short shrift" here.) From the vast treasury of our language, only a relatively minuscule number of phrases could be included here—trying to decide which to use and which to reject was one of my hardest problems. I may not always have chosen well.

A great many phrases made the list because they're known to have given problems to reporters and students in the past. For instance, you'd expect all reporters to know how to spell "en masse," but I saw it in a transcript a few months ago as "in mass." And you'll find "shudder to think" merely because I heard that one reporter wrote it as *"shutter* to think"!

The phrases chosen add up to a real potpourri. (Potpourri: one word.) I've read that of all the world's many languages, English is the richest in idiom. (If you haven't read "Our Native Idiom" and would like to, you'll find it in the Appendix.) This rich medley of idiom comprises more than half of the book, I suspect. Also, you'll find literary quotations, clichés (and usually the literary quote *is* now a cliché), quite a lot of Latin (mostly legal terms), a fair amount of French plus a few terms from other languages, a great deal of slang, a smattering of medical phrases, a few computer and other phrases of fairly recent origin, terms from the drug scene, even some Black English.

Definitions have necessarily been kept short. In fact, some rather well-known lines from literature needed no definition at all, I felt. Two things that appeared in the original *NSR* series have been dropped: diacritics (on foreign words) and pronunciations. After all, reporters' typewriters and CAT printers don't normally provide for diacritics.

If I had my druthers (yes, that phrase is included), I'd like to see this book serve two purposes: First and foremost (cliché not included), you hold in your hands a good little reference book. Though there are few entries in it that don't appear in *some* dictionary or other reference work, you may well find what you're looking for much faster here. As an example, a few years ago I had the expression "eeny, meeny, miney, mo" in a deposition. To save my transcriber some work, I thought I would quickly dig it out and add to my dog-sheet. Well, after looking in about five dictionaries, I finally found it in *Webster's Second,* unabridged. (It isn't in the *Third.*) Forgetting where I had earlier struck gold, I went through the same process again in seeking the correct spelling to include here.

Second, I hope you'll find the booklet rather fun to read—not straight through, but for browsing. (Where I've found interesting word or phrase origins, I've included them.) And, though I don't like to use this workaday word while talking about fun, dipping into the book might even be educational. That is, the phrase you encounter perhaps for the first time here may pop up in court tomorrow—or familiarity with some of these terms may help you pass NCRA's Written Knowledge Test.

Let me conclude by thanking two people: Lorraine Perry of NCRA headquarters, who typeset this booklet in-house on her trusty Wang word processor (and who showed great patience with me when I asked to add or alter entries); and Marvin P. Birnbaum, CM, who advised me when asked, helped track down some elusive definitions, and then aided in proofreading.

Mary Louise Gilman
Hanover, Mass.
1984

TABLE OF CONTENTS

Preface v
Fairly Familiar Phrases 1
Appendix
  "Our Native Idiom" 43
  Bibliography 47

A

ab initio—(L.) From the beginning.
abject terror—Panic.
Abominable Snowman—A large manlike or bearlike animal said to exist in the Himalayas; a yeti.
a capella—(It., lit. from the chapel) Without accompaniment.
accentuate the positive—From a song title.
accessory after the fact—One who knowingly aids after commission of a crime by sheltering the criminal, etc.
according to Hoyle—Adhering to prescribed rules and regulations. (Edmond Hoyle, who died in 1769, wrote an encyclopedia of card games.)
ac/dc—Bisexual.
ace in the hole—A secret reserve of strength. (A reserve card in stud poker, turned to the table.)
ace up one's sleeve—Something in reserve.
Achilles' heel—Vulnerable spot. (From the Greek legend.)
aching void—A sense of loss and emptiness.
Adam's off ox—"I wouldn't know him from Adam's off ox." (The off ox in a team of oxen is the one on the right, farthest from the driver.)
ad infinitum—(L.) Without limit.
ad-lib—To improvise words or actions.
ad nauseam—(L.) To the point of nausea. (Note spelling of the second word of this and of ad infinitum.)
aegis of, under the—See *under the aegis of.*
agent provocateur—(F.) Secret agent. (Pl.: agents provocateurs.)
a-go-go—A nightclub for dancing to pop music; discotheque.
aide-memoire—(F.) An aid to the memory; memorandum.

a la—(F.) In the manner of.
alarums and excursions—Clamor, excitement; feverish or disordered activity.
"Alas! poor Yorick. I knew him, Horatio."—Shakespeare's *Hamlet.* (Usually misquoted as "I knew him well.")
albatross around one's neck—A heavy cross to bear. (From *Rime of the Ancient Mariner* by Coleridge, 1798.)
al fresco—(It., lit. in the fresh) In the open air.
all chiefs and no Indians—All bosses and no workers.
all fours—See *on all fours.*
all get-out—To an extreme degree.
all that glitters is not gold—(Shakespeare, in *Merchant of Venice,* wrote "all that *glisters.*")
all things come to him who waits—Be patient. "All things come round to him who will but wait," Longfellow, *Tales of a Wayside Inn.* (We sometimes hear "to he who waits," which is atrocious grammar.)
alpha and omega—(Greek letters) The beginning and the end.
alter ego—(L., lit. another I) A second self; trusted friend.
altogether, in the—Nude.
amen corner—A conspicuous corner in a church occupied by fervent worshipers.
a mensa et thoro—(L.) From bed and board. (Lit., from table and bed. Sometimes heard in divorce cases.)
amicus curiae—(L.) Friend of the court.
amok (or amuck), run—(Malayan) To act in a murderous frenzy.
animus furandi—(L.) Intent to steal.
Annie Oakley—In memory of a famous riflewoman who could throw a playing card into the air and shoot it as full of holes as a punched meal ticket before it landed, this means a meal ticket, and, figuratively, any complimentary ticket or newspaperman's pass.—*Phrase and Word Origins,* Holt.
A-O.K.—Functioning very smoothly.

1

a posteriori—(L.) Inductive; derived from reasoning by observed facts.

apple-pie order—In perfect order.

apres moi le deluge—(F., lit. after me the deluge) Attributed usually to Louis XV, sometimes to Mme. de Pompadour.

a priori—(L.) Deductive; self-evident.

arm and a leg, an—An exorbitant price.

arms akimbo—With hands on hips and elbows pointed outward.

arm's length—A distance discouraging personal contact or familiarity; the condition or fact that parties to a transaction are independent and on an equal footing; e.g., an arm's-length transaction.

arms of Morpheus, in the—Asleep. Morpheus was the Greek god of dreams—from whom the word *morphine* comes to us.

around the bend—To have taken leave of one's senses, to have become irrational.

ass backwards—In the reverse order (vulgar).

at loggerheads—Engaged in a violent quarrel.

at sixes and sevens—See *sixes and sevens*.

au contraire—(F.) On the contrary.

au courant—(F., lit. with the current) Up to date, fully informed.

Augean stables (cleaning the)—Clearing away massive corruption or filth. Hercules performed the original task.

auld lang syne—(Sc.) The good old days.

au naturel—(F.) In the natural state; in the nude.

au pair—(F.) On equal terms (nowadays usually applied to girls working in another country, mostly as domestics).

autres temps, autres moeurs—(F.) Other times, other customs.

avant-garde—(F., vanguard) An intelligentsia that develops new or experimental concepts, esp. in the arts.

B

back and fill—To manage the sails of a ship to keep it clear of obstacles; to shilly-shally.

back burner, on the—Where one puts projects, etc., not under active consideration.

back to square one—See *square one*.

bad blood—Ill feeling or bitterness.

bad-mouth—To speak disparagingly of.

bad odor, in—Having unclean hands; in an unsavory situation.

baker's dozen—Thirteen.

bald-faced lie (also **bare-faced lie, bold-faced lie**)—A shameless lie.

balm of (or **in**) **Gilead**—Something that soothes, relieves, or heals.

Band-Aid approach (treatment, etc.)—Application of temporary or patched-up measures to a serious problem.

bare-faced lie—See *bald-faced lie*.

"Barkis is willin' "—A phrase indicating one's willingness. From *David Copperfield*, Dickens.

bark up the wrong tree—To direct attention wrongly.

bar mitzvah—(Y.) Confirmation (of a boy).

barrel, over a—At a disadvantage; in an awkward position.

basket case—One utterly worn out or incapacitated.

bated breath—Breathing subdued or restrained, under the influence of awe, terror, or other emotion. (One never *baits* one's breath!)

bat mitzvah—(Y.) Confirmation (of a girl).

bats in the belfry, to have—To be crazy or eccentric.

batten down the hatches—To make a boat, etc., safe from a storm; to secure with battens.

bawl out—To scold or chastise.

be-all and (the) end-all—The thing that matters more than anything else. From Shakespeare's *Macbeth*.

beard the lion in his den—To confront and oppose someone in his own stronghold.

beat about (or around) the bush—To be slow to come to the point. From hunting.

beat one's breast—See *breast-beating*.

beat the bushes—To search thoroughly in all possible areas.

beau geste—(F.) A graceful or magnanimous gesture.

beck and call, at one's—In obedient readiness to obey any command.

bedroom community—Said of a suburb in which many residents work in the city.

bee in one's bonnet—Usually suggests a fantastic idea or crazy notion. The phrase dates from 1648.

beef trust—A group of large or fat people, especially chorus girls.

beer and skittles (usu. **not all beer and skittles**)—Easygoing existence.

beetle-browed—With projecting brows; scowling.

beggars description—Defies description.

beg the question—To assume something not yet proved.

behind the eight ball—In a highly disadvantageous position.

belly-up—(Adj., position of a dead fish) Done for; in bankruptcy. (Verb, without hyphen) To move close or next to. (He bellied up to the bar.)

beside oneself—In a state of extreme excitement.

beside the point—Irrelevant.

best bib and tucker—One's best clothes (ca. 1747). A tucker is a piece of lace or cloth inserted in the front of a dress.

"best-laid schemes o' mice an' men / Gang aft agley"—Our plans often miscarry. From *To a Mouse*, Robert Burns.

bete noire—(F., lit. black beast) Disliked person or thing; nemesis, bugbear, stumbling block.

between a rock and a hard place—On the horns of a dilemma.

between Scylla and Charybdis—Between two equally hazardous alternatives.

betwixt and between—Neither one thing nor the other.

Bible Belt—An area chiefly in southern U.S. in which people are believed to take literally everything in the Bible.

billet-doux—(F.) Love letter.

bindle stiff—A migratory harvest worker; a hobo.

bird dog—(Noun) One, such as a talent scout, that seeks out something for another. (Verb, hyphenated) To seek out. (He bird-dogged the contract for us.)

blind-man's buff—A group game in which a blindfolded player tries to catch and identify another player. (Sometimes incorrectly heard as blind-man's *bluff*.)

blot on one's escutcheon—A stain on one's reputation.

blow one's cool—To lose one's composure.

blow one's cover—To reveal one's true identify.

blow one's mind—To overwhelm with wonder or bafflement.

blow one's stack (or top)—To become violently angry or even crazy.

blow smoke—To boast, brag, or exaggerate.

board, go by the—See *go by the board*.

body English—Twisting of the body during a game as if to help the ball travel in the desired path

bold-faced lie—See *bald-faced lie*.

bollixed up—Confused, mixed up.

bona fides—(L.) Honest intention; sincerity.

bone up on—To try to master necessary information quickly; to cram.

bon mot—(F.) Clever remark.

bonum per se—(L.) Good in itself.

bon vivant — (F.) One who lives well; gourmand.

boot, to — In addition. The Old English *bot* meant advantage, profit, compensation for injury.

borrow, ordinary — Material used as fill (often taken from a borrow pit). This can be confusing, since construction workers and contractors sometimes pronounce the word burrow.

borscht circuit (or **borscht belt**) — Summer vacation hotels in the Catskills (often applied to theaters).

bottom out, to — To reach a low point before rebounding. (As in the stock market.)

box the compass — To name the 32 points of the compass in their order; to make a complete reversal.

brain drain — Migration of professionals, such as physicians or engineers, to another country for economic reasons.

brazen (it) out — To proceed, after doing wrong, as if one had nothing to be ashamed of.

break stride — To hesitate or cease to function at desired speed or efficiency. (From horse racing.)

breast-beating — Noisy demonstrative protests as of grief, anger, self-incrimination. (In one well-publicized instance, a reporter transcribed this as *breast-feeding* !)

bred-in-the-bone — (Adj.) Deep-rooted.

bricks, hit the — To go on strike.

bright-eyed and bushy-tailed — Alert, ready for anything.

Bronx cheer — The old raspberry.

brown bagging — Carrying one's lunch in a paper bag; carrying a bottle into a restaurant where sale of liquor by the drink is illegal.

brown study, deep in a — Deep in thought.

bruit about (or **abroad**) — To report widely.

buff, in the — Nude.

bug out — To withdraw, retreat.

bull in a china shop — A person who acts in a gauche or tactless manner or even with violence.

burden of one's song — One's true meaning or conviction.

bush league — A minor league. (From baseball.)

butter wouldn't melt in her mouth — She is less demure and prim than she looks. This dates from 1781.

buy a pig in a poke — To buy unseen. (A poke is a sack. The Germans say "die Katze [cat] im Sack kaufen.")

by a long chalk (or **not by a long chalk**) — [Not] by any means; far from it. Chalk is used for scoring points (*Not by a long shot,* which means the same thing, is more commonly heard; but we need to be aware of both phrases.)

by and large — On the whole.

by leaps and bounds — Growing or progressing rapidly. (Not to be confused with "metes and bounds," a term used in describing land boundaries.)

by rule of thumb — A method of arriving at an approximate or commonsense result. (Lit. by using the thumb to measure.)

C

call in question — To doubt the truth of.

can of worms — Pandora's box.

can't hold a candle to — Is greatly inferior.

carrot-and-stick — (Adj.) The traditional alternatives of driving a donkey by holding out a carrot or beating it.

carry coals to Newcastle — To take a thing to a place where it is already plentiful.

carte blanche — (L.) With full power to act as one thinks best. (Lit., blank document.)

cast pearls before swine—To give something precious to those who are unable to appreciate it. *(Matthew 7:6.)*

casus belli—(L.) An action or event that justifies or allegedly justifies war or conflict.

catbird seat—Position of prominence or advantage.

catch-as-catch-can—(Adj.) Using any available means or method.

cater-cornered (catercorner, catty-corner, kitty-corner, kitty-cornered)—On a diagonal. [Note that *catercorner* isn't hyphenated.]

catholic tastes—Wide and varied tastes. (This has nothing to do with the Catholic church, but the word stems from a Greek word meaning universal, which applies in both cases.)

cat's cradle—A children's game played with a piece of string; something intricate.

cat's-paw—A dupe. (From the old fable of the monkey that used a cat's paw to draw chestnuts from the fire.)

causa mortis—(L.) In contemplation of approaching death.

cause celebre—(F.) A famous lawsuit, etc.

caveat emptor—(L.) Let the buyer beware.

caveat venditor—(L.) Let the seller beware.

c'est la guerre—(F.) That's war.

c'est la vie—(F.) That's life.

cestui que trust—He who has a right to a beneficial interest in and out of an estate the legal title to which is vested in another.

chacun a son gout—(F.) Each to his own taste.

chalk up—Ascribe; credit. (Chalk it up to experience.)

champ at the bit—To show impatience at delay or restraint.

chapter and verse—An exact reference to a passage or authority.

charge d'affaires—(F.) An ambassador's deputy.

charley horse—A muscular strain or bruise, esp. of the quadriceps, characterized by pain and stiffness.

cheap shot—An unfair statement that takes advantage of an opponent's weakness.

cherchez la femme!—(F.) Look for the woman [in the case].

Cheshire cat—A broadly grinning cat. (From *Alice in Wonderland.*)

chestnuts in the fire—Plans; schemes. [See *cat's paw.*]

chew the cud—To ruminate.

chew the fat (or rag)—To reminisce.

chicken out—To withdraw from a plan, task, or endeavor because of fear.

Chinaman's chance—A very small chance or none at all.

chin-wag—A conversation.

chip off the old block—A child who resembles his father.

chip on one's shoulder, to have—To be quarrelsome or belligerent.

choice of rotten apples—Pretty slim pickings. "There's small choice in rotten apples," Shakespeare, *Taming of the Shrew.*

chop-chop—[Pidgin Eng.] Without delay; quickly.

chose in action—A personal right not reduced into possession but recoverable by a suit at law. [Note that *chose* is pronounced like *shows.*]

clam up—To refrain from talking.

clear the decks—To prepare for action by removing all unessential material.

clerk of the works—Superintendent of a construction project.

cloud nine, on—Extremely happy.

clover, in—In luck; prosperous. The allusion is to cattle feeding in fields of clover.

C-note—A $100 bill.

cobbler should stick to his last—See *stick to one's last.*

cock-and-bull story—A canard; an elaborate lie.

cocked hat—See *knocked into.*

cock of the walk—One that dominates a group, etc., esp. overbearingly.

Code Napoleon—Code embodying the civil law of France.

coffee klatch—(Ger., *Kaffeeklatsch*, conversation over coffee) Usu. connotes a gossip session. (*Klatsch* means gossip.)

cold comfort—Poor consolation.

cold turkey—Sudden withdrawal of a drug (or tobacco) from an addict without preparation.

come a cropper—See *cropper.*

come full circle—To go through a series of events and return to the starting point. See also *wheel is come.*

come hell or high water—No matter what the obstacles.

comeuppance, to get one's—To receive a deserved rebuke or a downfall.

come up smelling like a rose—To emerge from an unsavory situation with one's reputation intact.

comme si, comme ca—(F.) So, so.

comparisons are odious—Or as Dogberry said *(Much Ado About Nothing)*, "Comparisons are odorous." The phrase predates Shakespeare.

compos mentis—(L.) Sound mind.

confusion worse confounded—Confusion added to confusion. (From Milton's *Paradise Lost.*)

consensus of opinion—General agreement. [Note: since *consensus* itself means general agreement, the phrase is redundant.]

consummation devoutly to be wished—An extremely desirable result. From Shakespeare's *Hamlet,* often misquoted as "devoutly to be desired."

Cook's tour—A quick tour, with only a cursory view of the attractions.

cop out—To back out or to evade. (The noun form is hyphenated: His failing to show up is a real cop-out.)

cordon bleu—(F.) Blue ribbon. A cordon bleu can also be a person of high rank or authority, esp. a cook of great skill.

cordon sanitaire—(F.) A chain of nations serving as a buffer against other aggressive nations.

corpus delicti—(L.) Lit., body of the crime; often used to refer to the body of a murder victim.

corpus juris—(L.) A body of law.

cotton-picking (or **cotton-pickin'**)—Common, vulgar, not valuable.

cotton to—To take a fancy to.

coup de grace—(F. lit. a stroke of grace) A finishing stroke; putting the end to a person's (or animal's) misery.

coup d'etat—(F.) A sudden decisive exercise of force in politics, such as the violent overthrow of a government.

cracked up—Highly praised. (This restaurant isn't all that it's cracked up to be.)

crash pad—Temporary lodging.

creature comforts—Food and other things for bodily comfort. The phrase dates from the 1600s.

creme de la creme—(F.) The very best, elite.

crocodile tears—Hypocritical tears or sympathy. (From an old story that a crocodile moans and sighs to attract the unwary traveler, then sheds tears as it devours him.)

cropper, come a—To have a bad fall or failure.

cross one's palms—(Usu. *with silver*) To pay, tip, or bribe.

cross the Rubicon—To commit oneself irrevocably. When Julius Caesar crossed the Rubicon River in 49 B.C., it was regarded as an act of war.

cry havoc—To alert to danger or disaster.

cry wolf—To give alarm unnecessarily. (From the old fable.)

cudgel one's brains—To think hard, to try to remember.

cudgels, take up—See *take up*.

cuff, off the—Without preparation; ad lib.

cuff, on the—On credit.

cul-de-sac—(F.) A blind passage; street closed at one end.

cum laude—(L.) With praise.

cup of tea—Something one likes or excels in.

curriculum vitae—(L.) An account of one's career and qualifications.

curry favor—To seek to gain favor by flattery or attention. (This was originally to curry *favel*—to rub down Favel, a horse in a 14th-century fable.)

cut above, a—A little better than.

cut and dried—Routine.

cut both ways—To result in simultaneous advantages and disadvantages.

cut no ice—To have no influence or effect.

cut off one's nose to spite one's face—To commit, through revenge or spite, some foolish action that injures oneself.

cut of one's jib—One's appearance, style, or manner. From sailing.

cut one's eyeteeth—To gain experience.

cut the Gordian knot—To solve a problem forcefully or by some unexpected means.

cut the mustard—To achieve the standard of performance necessary for success.

cynosure of all eyes—Since *cynosure* means center of attraction or attention, the expression is not only a cliché but redundant.

D

dago red—Cheap red wine.

Dame Grundy—See *Mrs. Grundy*.

damn with faint praise—To condemn with praise so moderate as to be no praise at all.

Damocles' sword—See *sword of Damocles*.

dander up, get one's—To become angry or concerned.

data base (or **data bank**)—A collection of data organized for rapid search and retrieval by a computer. (We sometimes see *database*, but the dictionary shows it as two words.)

Davy Jones's locker—At the bottom of the sea; drowned.

day one—From the beginning.

dead as a dodo—See *dodo*.

dead as a doornail—Quite dead. (Dead as a coffin nail would make more sense.)

dead in the water—Not going anywhere—e.g., a ship that has lost its power while at sea.

dead reckoning—Guesswork.

dead to rights—1. Certain. 2. Caught in the act or irrefutably accused of a crime, etc.

Dear John (letter)—A letter of dismissal from one's mate or sweetheart.

de bene esse—(L.) Conditionally; provisionally; in anticipation of need.

decree nisi—A provisional decree.

deep six—(Noun) A grave. (Verb, with hyphen) To throw away or discard, esp. embarrassing or incriminating material.

de facto—(L.) In fact; in reality; actually.

de gustibus non est disputandum—(L.) There's no accounting for tastes.

deja vu—(F.) The illusion of remembering scenes and events experienced for the first time.

de jure—(L.) By right.

de minimis non curat lex—(L.) The law does not concern itself with trifles.

de mortuis nil nisi bonum—(L.) Of the dead (say) nothing but good.

de novo—(L.) Anew; afresh; a second time.

de rigueur—(F.) It's a must.

derring-do—Daring action. (Originally from daring to do.)

de trop—(F.) Too much or too many; superfluous, unwanted.

deus ex machina—(L.) A person or thing (as in a drama) that appears suddenly to resolve an apparently insoluble difficulty.

devil-may-care—(Adj.) Cheerful and reckless.

devil's advocate—A person who champions a less accepted cause for the sake of argument.

devil take the hindmost—To hell with the consequences.

dibs on (something)—An expression used in claiming the next use of, or chance at, something.

Dick's hatband, queer as or **odd as**—Peculiar; strange.

die is cast, the—The decision has been irrevocably made. [Note that *die* is the singular form of *dice*.]

dime bag—$10 worth of drugs.

diminishing returns (sometimes **law of**)—A rate of yield that fails to increase in proportion to amount of labor or capital invested.

dirty laundry (or **linen**)—Private matters whose exposure can bring embarrassment.

dirty pool—Underhanded or unsportsmanlike conduct.

dish of tea—One's preference. (City life is not my dish of tea.)

distaff side—The female side of the family.

divvy up—To divide up.

doctor the accounts (or **figures**)—To falsify them.

dodo, dead as a—Past reviving. (The dodo is an extinct bird.)

dog-eared—Said of a book with turned-down corners of pages; shabby, worn.

dog eat dog—Marked by ruthless self-interest.

dolce vita—(It.) Lit., sweet life; a life of indolence and self-indulgence.

doldrums, in the—Depressed; down in the dumps.

domino effect—A cumulative effect brought about when one event produces a succession of similar events.

domino theory—A theory that if one nation (as in S.E. Asia) falls to the Communists, the domino effect will cause neighboring nations to follow suit.

donkey's years—A very long time.

don't get your dander up—See *dander*.

do one proud—To treat lavishly or with honor; to make someone feel proud. (Our performance here does us proud.)

do-or-die—(Adj.) Doggedly determined to reach one's objectives.

do-re-mi—Money.

dot the i's and cross the t's—To be minutely accurate and explicit about details.

double blind—(Adj.) An experimental procedure in which neither subjects nor experimenters know the makeup of the test and the control groups during the experiment.

double-digit—Amounting to 10 percent or more (as double-digit inflation).

double entendre—(F.) Double meaning, usually risqué.

double in brass—To be versatile or to get income from two sources. Originally from dance-orchestra slang.

double in spades—That goes double; you can say that again. (Sometimes heard simply as *in spades*. This phrase apparently comes from the game of pinochle, in which points scored have double value when spades are trump.)

doubting Thomas—A habitually doubtful person.

down-at-the-heel(s)—(Adj.) Shabby.

down in the mouth—Looking or being unhappy.

down the drain (or **pipe** or **tube**)—All three expressions mean the same thing, though the first one is the oldest.

down to the wire—Down to the finish line. (From horse racing.)

Draconian measures—Severe or cruel measures.

draggle-tail—(Noun) A slovenly person.

dramatis personae—(L.) Characters in a drama.

draw a bead on—To take aim at. The "bead" is the front side of a firearm.

drawing board(s), back to the—A return to the planning stage.

dress down—(1) To reprove severely. (A dressing down is about the same as a bawling out.) (2) To dress casually—opposite of dress up.

dressed to the nines—Dressed very elaborately.

dribs and drabs—Small amounts.

drug on the market—A commodity for which there is no demand. (Says Holt: "This *drug* is perhaps from the French *drogue*, meaning obsolete.")

druthers, if I had my—If I had my choice.

dry behind the ears—See *not dry*.

dry run—Rehearsal.

ducks and drakes—The pastime of skimming stones, etc., along the surfaces of calm water. To play ducks and drakes with, or to make ducks and drakes of, is to use recklessly; squander.

duck soup—Something easy; a person who is a pushover.

dudgeon, high—See *high dudgeon*.

duffel bag—A large cloth or canvas bag.

dull as ditch water (or **dishwater**)—Pretty dull.

dummy up—To refuse to talk; to clam up.

dump on—To bad-mouth.

dunk shot—See *slam dunk*.

durance vile, in—Imprisoned.

Dutch courage—Courage produced by strong drink.

Dutch uncle—Someone, usually a man, who talks to one severely.

dyed-in-the-wool—(Adj.) Thoroughgoing, uncompromising.

E

early on—Fairly early. (A phrase borrowed from the British.)

ear to the ground, to have one's—To be alert to rumors and trends of opinion.

easy virtue—Sexually promiscuous behavior or habits.

eat crow, to—Bergen Evans wrote that the expression was at first "to eat boiled crow." To eat one, he said, "would be a disgusting experience, and to have to eat one in public would be humiliating."

eat high off (or **on**) **the hog**—To live well. "The expression is quite literally accurate, since you have to go pretty high on the hog to get the tender—and expensive—loin chops and roasts." [William and Mary Morris.]

eat humble pie—To apologize humbly.

edge on, to have an—To have an advantage over a person.

eeny, meeny, miney, mo—The first line of a child's counting-out rhyme.

egg on—To urge on.

egg on one's face, with—In a state of embarrassment or humiliation.

ego trip—Something that enhances one's ego.

eight ball—See *behind the*.

elbow bending—Drinking liquor.

elbow grease—Hard work.

elementary, my dear Watson—From *Sherlock Holmes,* by A. Conan Doyle.

eleventh hour—The last moment. (Of Biblical origin.)

El Nino—(S., the boy) An intermittent warm current that appears and disappears in the Pacific and is thought to have a great effect on California's weather.

embarrassment of riches—Too much of something.

en banc—(F., on the bench) The full court.

en bloc—(F.) In a bloc or as a unit.

end of one's tether—See *tether*.

enfant terrible—(F.) A terrifying child; person whose rash conduct and inopportune remarks cause embarrassment.

en masse—(F.) All together; wholesale.

en passant—(F.) In passing; incidentally.

entre nous—(F.) Just between us; confidentially.

espirit de corps—(F.) The common spirit pervading members of a body or association.

et alius—(L.) And another; et al. is the abbreviation. (Plural: et alii, also abbreviated et al. or sometimes et als.)

et tu, Brute!—(L.) Thou also, Brutus—exclamation attributed to Julius Caesar when stabbed by his best friend, Brutus. Hence, an accusation of treachery from one's intimate friend.

et uxor—(L.) And wife; et ux. the abbrev.

euchered out of—Cheated; tricked. (Euchre is a card game.)

even Steven—An even score. The source may be Swift's *Letters to Stella:* " 'Now we are even,' quoth Steven, when he gave his wife six blows to one."

even tenor of one's ways (pursuing the)—To go quietly and steadily on. From Gray's *Elegy in a Country Churchyard,* 1751.

every now and then—Occasionally. (Though some people may say "*ever* now and then," it should be considered a mispronunciation.)

every once in a while—Occasionally. (See previous phrase.)

every so often—Occasionally. (Not to be confused with "*ever* so often," which means frequently and repeatedly; but many people will omit the final syllable when they *mean* "every so often.")

ex cathedra—(L.) From the seat of authority.

exception that proves the rule—Most authorities agree that this expression originally meant (and still should) an exception that *tests* the rule.

eyeteeth, to give one's—Willing to pay the price.

F

fail-safe—To revert to a danger-free condition in the event of a breakdown or other failure.

"Faint heart ne'er won fair lady"—*Don Quixote,* by Cervantes.

fair shake—A fair chance or fair treatment.

fair to middling—Just average; tolerable.

fait accompli—(F., lit. accomplished fact) A thing accomplished and presumably irreversible.

fall all over oneself—1. To be very awkward. 2. To be very hasty or eager.

fall between two stools—To fail because of inability to choose between or reconcile two alternatives of conflicting courses of action.

falsus in uno, falsus in omnibus—(L.) False in one thing, false in everything.

familiar spirit—A spirit or demon that serves or prompts an individual.

fancy-schmancy—Derogatory term with a Yiddish flavor.

far and away—By a considerable margin.

far be it from me—May I never; I neither hope nor dare.

far cry from—Greatly different from.

fare-thee-well or **fair-you-well**—The utmost degree.

far from the madding crowd—Far from the insane turmoil of crowds. (Gray's *Elegy*, 1751.) Sometimes misquoted as *maddening* crowd.

fat chance—No chance at all.

fat farm—A resort for people who wish to lose weight.

fat's in the fire, the—The damage is done.

fault, to a—In excess. (He was generous to a fault.)

faux pas—(F., lit. a false step) Embarrassing mistake.

feel one's oats—Lively, full of energy. (A horse who is full of oats is frisky.) To *sow one's wild oats* is something entirely different.

fee simple—A fee without limitation to any class of heirs or restrictions on ownership.

feet of clay—A flaw of character that is not usually apparent.

fell swoop, at one—See *one fell swoop*.

femme fatale—(F., lit. fatal woman.) A seductive woman who lures men into dangerous or compromising situations.

field day—A time of extraordinary pleasure or opportunity.

fifth wheel—One that is superfluous, unnecessary, or burdensome.

fine fettle—In good health and spirits. The Old English word *fetel* meant belt—a properly belted man felt ready to take on all comers in battle.

fine kettle of fish—See *kettle of fish*.

fine-tooth comb—An attitude or system of thorough searching or scrutinizing.

finger in the dike—Use of desperate emergency measures, usu. of limited effectiveness.

fink out—To fail miserably; to back out, cop out.

first blood—The first success in a contest.

first water, of the—Of the finest quality. From diamond testing.

fish or cut bait—To make an immediate choice between two alternatives; esp. to join in some work scheme or be left out of consideration.

fits and starts, by—In an impulsive and irregular manner.

flagrante delicto—See *in flagrante delicto*.

flash in the pan—A sudden spasmodic effort that accomplishes nothing. (It originated in the days of the flintlock muskets.)

flea in one's ear—An irritating hint or warning.

flora and fauna—Plant and animal life (of a region).

flotsam and jetsam—Wreckage either floating or washed up on shore; often applied to humanity's derelicts.

flub the dub—To evade one's duty; to ruin.

fly in the face of Providence—To ignore good advice; to tempt fate.

fly in the ointment—Some small object or trifling circumstance that lessens one's enjoyment of a thing. (*Ecclesiastes 10:1*: "Dead flies cause the ointment . . . to send forth a stinking savour.")

fob off—To pass or offer (something spurious) as genuine.

Foggy Bottom—A district in Washington, D.C.; the U.S. State Department.

fogy, old—See *old fogy*.

for auld lang syne: For old time's sake. (*Auld Lang Syne*, Burns, 1789)

forma pauperis—See *in forma pauperis*.

foul one's own nest—To commit a sin or fault that will ruin one's home, etc. From an old proverb about a bird.

four sheets to (or **in**) **the wind**—Drunk.

Fourth Estate—The public press. (Now sometimes applied to all news media.) It was "coined ca. 1790, perhaps by Burke," says Eric Partridge.

"Frailty, thy name is woman!"—Shakespeare's *Hamlet*.

Frankenstein's monster—Any agency or creation that slips from the control of and ultimately destroys its creator. From Mary W. Shelley's novel, *Frankenstein*. Though the creator was Frankenstein the man, we now frequently hear the unnamed *monster* called Frankenstein.

freak-out—(Noun) A withdrawal from reality. (Don't hyphenate the verb form.)

free-for-all—A fight or discussion in which anyone may join.

French leave—To take French leave is to go AWOL. (In 17th-century France it was proper to leave a party early without bidding farewell to host or hostess.)

Freudian slip—An unintentional error that seems to reveal subconscious feelings.

fritter away—To diminish or reduce piecemeal. Alfred H. Holt says it is related to *fracture*—to break yourself into such small pieces that you are quite wasted.

fritz, on the—In a state of disrepair. William and Mary Morris suggest the phrase originated with Hans and Fritz of the comic strip "Katzenjammer Kids."

from Dan to Beersheba—From limit to limit; throughout the whole region. From *Judges 20:1*—the 150 miles from one end of the Holy Land to the other.

from scratch (or **start from scratch**)—From the beginning. (She makes cookies from scratch rather than from a prepared mix.)

from time immemorial—See *time immemorial*.

fruit salad—Ribbons and other decorations on a uniform (e.g., worn by an Army general).

full circle—See *come full circle* and *wheel is come*.

full of beans—Full of health and spirits.

full of moxie—High-spirited. (From Moxie, a soft drink.)

full stop—Period (British).

full tilt—High speed.

G

gall and wormwood—Something extremely bitter.

galley-west—Into destruction or confusion. (It knocked his plans galley-west.)

gallows humor—Humor that makes fun of a serious or terrifying situation.

game is not worth the candle—The effort is not worth making.

gamut, run the—See *run the gamut*.

garden path, lead down the—To entice; to mislead deliberately.

garden variety—Average or ordinary.

gauntlet, run the—See *run the gauntlet*.

gauntlet, throw down the—See *throw down the gauntlet*.

gave up the ghost—Died. (*Luke 23:46.*)

gentleman's (or **gentlemen's**) **agreement**—One that is binding in honor but not enforceable by law.

get cracking—To make a start; get going.

get off—To get high on a drug; to have an orgasm.

get one's back up—To take offense. (The allusion is to a cat, which arches its back when frightened or angry.)

get-up-and-go—Energy displayed.

get up to speed—To become thoroughly familiar with something (not just one's shorthand system!).

get wind of—To become aware of.

gild the lily—A misquotation from Shakespeare (*King John*). Correct: "To gild refined gold, to paint the lily/To throw perfume on the violet . . ." See *paint the lily*.

gird one's loins—To prepare for action.

give a wide berth to—To avoid sedulously.

give no quarter—To show an opponent no clemency.

give pause to—To cause to hesitate.

give the lie to—To refute vigorously; to prove the falsity of.

give up the ghost—See *gave up the ghost.*

glad hand—A warm welcome or greeting, often prompted by ulterior reasons.

glad rags—Dressy clothes.

glom on to—To take possession of.

go begging—To be in little demand.

go by the board—To be lost, abandoned, finally or fully. (Lit., to fall overboard.)

go down to the wire—See *down to the wire.*

go great guns—To proceed vigorously or at full speed.

go farther (or **further**) **and fare worse**—Not content with something available or offered, to pass on and experience bad fortune or inferior treatment. (Usu. "You could well go farther and fare worse.")

go for broke—To put forth all one's strength or resources.

go hat in hand—To go obsequiously, to plead or intercede—with head uncovered, to show respect.

good old (or **ole**) **boy**—A usu. rural white Southerner who conforms to the behavior of his peers.

goody-goody—(Adj.) Smugly virtuous.

go off the deep end—To get very excited; to become mentally unstable.

goon squad—A group of thugs, esp. when employed in labor disputes.

Gordian knot—See *cut the Gordian knot.*

gorge rises at, one's—One feels extremely disgusted at or resentful of. (*Hamlet.*)

go to the mat—See *mat.*

go to the wall—Says Alfred H. Holt, "Already in the 16th century, 'up against it,' to be bankrupt or put on the shelf."

go whole hog—To go the limit. Says Holt, "While Stevenson looks with favor on the theory that the Irish nickname 'hog' for a shilling may have been the source (i.e., 'spend the whole shilling'), OED prefers the story about the pious but hungry Mohammedans, who had been ordered by their leader not to eat some unspecified part of a pig. Having no way of determining which part was intended, they ate the whole business."

grass roots—Society at the local level, esp. in rural areas.

graveyard shift—A work shift beginning late at night.

gravy train—A much exploited source of easy money.

grease monkey—A mechanic, esp. on a car or plane.

greasy spoon—A small cheap usu. unsanitary restaurant.

green-eyed monster—Jealousy. (Shakespeare's *Othello.*)

grim reaper—Death.

grist for one's mill—Something put to one's advantage.

gum-beating—(Black Eng.) Talking.

gung-ho—Eager, enthusiastic (sometimes foolishly so). From a Chinese phrase meaning "working together."

gussied up—Dressed in one's best clothes.

H

hack it—To manage successfully; to tolerate.

hail and farewell—Hello and goodbye.

hail-fellow-well-met—(Adj.) Heartily friendly and congenial. ("Hail, fellow, well met,/All dirty and wet ...." Swift, 1765.)

hail from—To be or to have been a native or resident of.

hairbreadth escape—A very narrow escape.

hair of the dog that bit you—Another drink as a cure for a hangover. This phrase has been known since 1546, and refers to an ancient practice of using burnt hair of a dog as an antidote to its bite.

hair-raising—Descriptive of a story, etc., that would make one's hair stand on end.

hair shirt—A shirt made of rough animal hair worn next to the skin as penance.

halcyon days—Days that are quiet and calm; days of fine weather occurring near the winter solstice; a period of peace and tranquility.

hale and hearty—Robust.

half-cocked—(Adj.) Lacking adequate preparation or forethought. (Don't go off half-cocked.)

half-life—The time it takes the radioactivity of a substance to fall to half its original value.

halo effect—When one good quality or trait can evoke an overly favorable evaluation of the whole.

hammer and tongs—(Adv.) With great force, vigor, or violence.

hand in glove (or **hand and glove**)—In an extremely close relationship.

hand-me-down—An article of secondhand clothing.

hand over fist—Quickly and in large amounts.

hand-to-mouth—(Adj.) Having or providing nothing to spare. (He led a hand-to-mouth existence.)

hang by a thread (or **hair**)—To be in a very precarious position. See *sword of Damocles.*

hang fire—To delay or hesitate. (From firearms: to be slow in the explosion of a charge after the hammer falls.)

hanky-panky—Trickery, dishonest dealing; sexual dalliance.

hara-kiri—A messy form of suicide. (It's a Japanese term, lit. "a cutting of the belly," seldom used by the Japanese themselves.) Also spelled *hari-kari.*

hard-bitten—Seasoned by difficult experience; tough.

hard by—Near.

hard-nosed—Stubborn, tough.

hard put—Barely able. (He was hard put to find an answer.)

hare-brained—Giddy, flighty.

hark back to—To turn back to an earlier subject or time.

harum-scarum—Reckless, irresponsible.

hasta la vista—(S.) Good-bye.

hatchet job—A forceful or malicious attack.

hatchet man—A person hired for murder, coercion, or attack; one who agrees to do someone else's dirty work, such as firing an employee.

hat in hand—In an attitude of respectful humility.

haut monde—(F.) High society.

have at—To go to or deal with; to attack. (This phrase appears in Shakespeare.)

have the jump on—To have an advantage over.

havoc, cry (play, wreak)—See *cry havoc, play havoc, wreak havoc.*

hawk from a handsaw—"I am but mad north-northwest: when the wind is southerly I know a hawk from a handsaw."—*Hamlet.* (Often used in the negative: "he doesn't know a hawk from a handsaw.") Authorities differ: some say "handsaw" is a corruption of "heronshaw," a heron; others suggest that "hawk" is a plasterer's tool or comes from the Dutch "hauck," a carpenter's square.

head shop—A shop specializing in articles of interest to drug users.

heave-ho—Dismissal.

heebie-jeebies—Jitters, willies.

heel, down at the—See *down at the heel.*

heir apparent—One who inherits or is likely to inherit property or to succeed in title.

heir presumptive—An heir whose legal right to an inheritance may be defeated, as by the birth of a child.

hell and gone—Irretrievably lost; describing a remote place.

hell-bent—Stubbornly determined. (Often heard as hell-bent for election.)

hell-bent for leather—At full speed.

hell has no fury like a woman scorned—An adaptation of Congreve's "Heaven has no rage like love to hatred turn'd/Nor hell a fury like a woman scorned." (Often further misquoted as "hell hath no fury . . . .")

hell or high water—See *come hell*.

helter-skelter—In disorderly confusion.

hepped up—(Usu. with *all*) Highly excited.

hide one's light under a bushel—To conceal one's merit or abilities. The allusion comes from *Matthew 5:15*.

hide or (nor) hair—A vestige or trace of someone or something.

higgledy-piggledy—In confusion; topsy-turvy.

high-and-mighty—(Adj.) Arrogant, imperious.

high dudgeon—A state or fit of indignation.

highest and best use—This splendid phrase, which is self-explanatory, is heard in eminent domain (condemnation) cases.

high-flown—Having extravagant ways; pompous (of language).

high-handed—Arbitrary, arrogant.

high horse, on one's—Behaving with pretentiousness or arrogance.

high jinks—A boisterous good time; horseplay.

high mucky muck (or **high-muck-a-muck**)—A person of high station or authority, who likes to impress others with his importance.

high off the hog—See *eat high*.

high roller—A big gambler.

high-water mark—The level reached at high water; the highest point or value.

hill (or **row**) **of beans**—Of little importance.

his nibs—An important person.

hit man—Hatchet man.

hit or miss—Haphazard. (Unfortunately, we often hear this as "hit *and* miss," which makes little sense—either you hit it or you miss it.)

hit the fan—To have a major usu. undesirable impact. (Cleaned-up version.)

Hobson's choice—No choice at all; an enforced decision.

hocus-pocus—Sleight of hand.

hog-tie—To tie together the feet of; to make helpless.

hog-wild—Lacking in restraint of judgment or temper.

hoi polloi, the—The multitude; the populace. From the Greek.

hoist on (properly **with**) **one's own petard**—Caught in one's own trap. From *Hamlet*. (The word *petard*, now usually defined as an explosive, comes from a French word meaning to break wind.)

hoity-toity—Arrogant, pompous, pretentious.

hold a candle to—See *can't hold a candle to*.

holding one's own—To maintain one's ground or position.

hold no brief for—To disclaim advocacy of.

hold sway—To have a dominant influence; rule.

hold water—To bear close scrutiny. (His argument doesn't hold water.)

hold with—To agree with or approve of.

hole card—A card in stud poker dealt face down and seen only by the player; any concealed asset.

hole up—To hide oneself.

holier-than-thou—(Adj.) Self-righteous.

home in on—To go to the source of; to target. [Note: the verb *hone*, which means to sharpen or whet, is sometimes erroneously used in this sense.]

Homer sometimes nods—Even the best of us can make mistakes.

Homo sapiens—The *genus* man.

honor among thieves—Could be part of the code of the underworld.

honor bound—Under a moral obligation to do something.

15

honored in the breach—See *more honored.*
hook, line, and sinker—Entirely.
hornet's nest—A troublesome or hazardous situation; an angry altercation.
horns of a dilemma, on the—Confronted with equally awkward alternatives—a vastly overworked phrase.
hors de combat—(F.) Out of the fight.
hors d'oeuvre—(F., plural hors d'oeuvres) An appetizer.
horse of another color—A thing significantly different.
house afire (or **house on fire**)—See *like a house afire.*
how-de-do—An awkward state of affairs. ("Here's a pretty how-de-do!" *The Mikado,* Gilbert and Sullivan.)
how the land lies (or **lays**)—What the situation is.
hue and cry—A loud outcry; hubbub.
hugger-mugger—(Adj.) Secret; confused or disorderly.
humble pie—See *eat humble pie.*
hunker down—To crouch, squat.
hurly-burly—(Noun) Uproar; tumult. (Adj.) Full of noise or confusion.
hurrah, last—See *last hurrah.*
hurrah's nest—A state of utmost confusion. No one seems to know what sort of a bird the hurrah is.

I

idee fixe—(F.) A fixed idea; obsession; prejudice.
ides of March—March 15th. "Beware the ides of March," from Shakespeare's *Julius Caesar.* (March 15th was the date predicted for Caesar's death.)
if I had it to do over again—If given a second chance. We sometimes hear this as "If I had to do it over again," which would literally mean "if *forced* to do it again" and usually isn't what the speaker means.

if I had my druthers—See *druthers.*
if push comes to shove—If it comes to that.
if the creek (crick) don't rise—Barring accidents.
if the worst comes to the worst—Says Alfred H. Holt, "What sense does that make? Why not say, with Robinson Crusoe, 'If the *worse comes to the worst'?*"Bergan Evans says of this cliché, "It is better to say *If it comes to the worst* or *If the worst happens."* (Of course, as reporters we report what people say.)
ignorance is bliss—From Gray's *Hymn to Adversity,* 1742, "where ignorance is bliss,/'Tis folly to be wise."
ill-starred—Unlucky.
ills that flesh is heir to, the (thousand)—"A misquotation of Shakespeare's *[Hamlet]* 'the thousand natural shocks that flesh . . .' " Eric Partridge.
ill wind that blows nobody good, it's an—From the days when all ships were propelled by use of sail; regardless of the wind's direction, it would benefit a ship somewhere. (Who was it who said of the oboe, "It's an ill wind that nobody blows good"?)
in camera—(L.) Lit., in a chamber; in secret.
in cold blood—It's the murderer, not the victim, whose blood is cold. "In hot blood" means under the influence of strong emotion.
Indian giver—An Americanism, which originally meant that the giver expected something in return but now means a gift snatched back from the recipient.
in durance vile—In prison. Partridge says, "It occurs first, so far as we know, in *Falstaff's Wedding,* by Wm. Kendrick (1777)."
in esse—(L.) In existence; in actuality.
in extenso—(L.) At full length.
in extremis—(L.) In the last illness.

in flagrante delicto—(Caught) unmistakably in the crime. "The Latin original seems to have been *flagrante delicto* ('while the crime is blazing'),'' Partridge tells us.

in for a penny, in for a pound—Once a thing is started, it must be carried through.

in forma pauperis—(L.) In the character or manner of a pauper; permission given a poor person to sue without liability for costs.

in futuro—(L.) In the future.

in haec verba—(L.) In these words.

in hoc—(L.) In this; in respect to this.

in jure—(L.) In law, according to law.

in light of (or **in the light of**)—In view of. A favorite phrase of lawyers, used both with and without *the*.

in like Flynn—Has breached the inner circle; has it made.

in line (or **on line**)—In most parts of America, people wait *in* line, but in New York they're more likely to wait *on* line. (In Britain they simply queue up.)

in loco parentis—(L.) In the place of a parent. (It has, of course, nothing to do with driving a parent nuts.)

in perpetuity—Forever.

in personem—(L.) Against a person.

in propria persona—(L.) Personally, and not by deputy or agents.

in rem—(L.) Against a thing. (An action in rem is against property, etc., rather than a person.)

in situ—(L.) In its original place.

in spades—See *double in spades.*

in statu quo—(L.) In the former or same state.

inter alia—(L.) Among other things.

inter alios—(L.) Between other persons.

inter nos—(L.) Between us.

in thrall—In bondage or slavery. Since it can also mean in a state of complete absorption, it should not be confused with *enthralled.*

in toto—(L.) Entirely; altogether.

in vino veritas—(L.) In wine there is truth.

ipso facto—(L.) By the very fact of.

iron out the bugs—Squish! (If you're saying it yourself, better make it *work* out the bugs.)

irons in the fire—Enterprises, undertakings.

ish kabibble—I should worry. (Outmoded phrase sometimes still heard.)

itching (or **itchy**) **foot**—A craving for travel.

itching (or **itchy**) **palm**—Shakespeare used the phrase in *Julius Caesar.* (This malady can usually be cured by crossing the palm with silver.)

it's an ill wind that blows nobody good—See *ill wind.*

itty-bitty (or **itsy-bitsy**)—Tiny.

ivory tower—Says John Ciardi, in *A Browser's Dictionary,* "The now standard symbol for the artificial world of ideas into which esthetic dreamers and impractical intellectuals are supposed to escape from the 'reality' of stockbrokers at a four-martini lunch."

Ivy League—Describing the first-founded U.S. colleges (Brown, Columbia, Cornell, Harvard, Princeton, Yale, etc.), based on the ivy-covered walls of these schools.

J

jack-in-the-box—A small box out of which a figure (as of a clown's head) springs when the lid is raised.

jack-of-all-trades—(Often followed by: and master of none.) A person who can do passable work at various tasks.

jai alai—A type of handball.

jaundiced eye—From *jaune* (F.), yellow. A prejudiced eye, which sees only faults. To take a jaundiced view is to regard with jealousy, envy, suspicion, or distrust.

Jekyll and Hyde—A person with a dual personality, one good, one evil. (From the story by Robert Louis Stevenson.)

je ne sais quoi—(F.) Lit., I know not what. Something that can't be described or explained.

jerkwater town—A primitive small town. "Originally a town on the railroad line, but too backward to have even a water tower. . . . The train crew had to 'jerk' water from the local wells and haul it laboriously to the locomotive." Ciardi.

jerry-built—Cheaply built, unsubstantial. Most authorities agree that "jerry" here is a corruption of "jury," as in "jury rig" or "jury mast," meaning something contrived for emergency or temporary use.

jib, cut of—See *cut of one's jib*.

jig is up, the—The project, etc., has failed. ("Jig," in British slang, means trick or fraud.)

jig time, in—Quickly.

Job, patience of—See *patience of Job*.

John Hancock (or **John Henry**)—John Hancock's signature on the Declaration of Independence was so much bigger and bolder than the others that it has become synonymous with "signature."

Johnny-come-lately—A newcomer.

Johnny-on-the-spot—One who is ready to help, esp. in an emergency.

joie de vivre—(F.) Joy of living.

jot or tittle—(Usually in the negative: not a jot or tittle) Not even a tiny bit. ("Till heaven and earth pass, one jot or tittle shall in no wise pass from the law, till all be fulfilled." Matthew 5:18.)

Judas kiss—A deceitful act of simulated affection.

judgment call—An on-the-spot decision (from the sports world).

jump ship—To desert one's ship.

jump the gun—To do anything prematurely (from racing).

jury-rig—To erect or arrange in makeshift fashion. [Quite different from a rigged jury!]

just deserts—What one deserves, whether good or bad. [Note: Though *deserts* here is accented on the second syllable, it should not be confused with *desserts*.]

just growed—"Like Topsy, it just growed" has been a staple American idiom for more than a century, says the *Harper Dictionary of Contemporary Usage*. Topsy, in *Uncle Tom's Cabin*, put it this way: "I 'spect I growed. Don't think nobody never made me."

K

kangaroo court—A mock court in which the principles of law and justice are disregarded or perverted.

keep a weather eye open (or **out**)—To watch out for.

keeping up with the Joneses—From a comic strip by I. Bacheller, ca. 1911. [Note: the only correct plural of *Jones* is *Joneses*.]

keep one's distance—To stay aloof.

keep one's eye peeled—To be alert.

keep one's hand in—To stay in practice.

kettle of fish—Bad state of affairs or predicament. (Usu. preceded by *fine* or *pretty*.)

kibosh on—See *put the kibosh on*.

kick over the traces—To shake off restraint or control.

kick the bucket—To die.

kick the gong around—To smoke opium (or sometimes marijuana).

kid gloves, handle or **treat with**—To give special consideration to.

kilter, out of—Not working properly.

kindred spirit—A person with interests or tastes similar to one's own.

kissing (kissin') cousin—Not a cousin by blood but almost a member of the family.

kit and caboodle—All of it; the whole shebang. *Kit* may refer to persons (as in *kith*), and *caboodle* seems to be related to *boodle*, meaning estate, goods, and chattels.

18

kith and kin—Friends and relatives. Thomas Middleton wrote in 1620, "A maid that's neither kith nor kin to me."

kitty-corner (or **kitty-cornered**)—See *cater-cornered*.

knee-high to a grasshopper—Very short, tiny. (U.S.)

knee-jerk—(Adj.) Readily predictable. (This aroused a knee-jerk reaction.)

knit one's brows—To frown.

knock-down-drag-out or **knock-down-and-drag-out**—Marked by bitterness or violence.

knocked for a loop—Overcame.

knocked into a cocked hat—Defeated.

knocked up—Pregnant.

knock off—To steal someone's product by making a cheap imitation. (The noun, knockoff, is one word.) This is a very versatile phrase. It also means (1) to discontinue, stop; (2) to deduct (knock off a few dollars from the price); (3) to kill (knock off two of the enemy's men); (4) to overcome or defeat (knock off each center of rebellion); (5) to rob (knock off a couple of banks).

knock the spots off of—To defeat badly.

knuckle down—To work hard.

knuckle under—To give in, submit.

kosher, not—See *not kosher*.

"Yes, knee jerk was definitely excessive."

L

labor of love—Work undertaken for the love of it, without pay.

lace-curtain—(Adj.) Prosperous, well-to-do. (Usu. heard in the phrase "lace-curtain Irish," which is considered somewhat offensive.)

la-di-da—Affected, pretentious.

lady of the evening—A prostitute.

laissez-faire—(F.) A doctrine opposing government interference in economic affairs.

lamb to slaughter, to lead—To victimize an easy prey.

lam, take it on the—See *take it on the lam*.

lame duck—An elected official who continues to hold office until the person elected to succeed him takes office.

land-office business—A briskly flourishing business.

lapsus linguae—(L.) A slip of the tongue.

last-ditch (effort, etc.)—Final desperate attempt.

last hurrah—A last effort or try. (From the book of the same name by Edwin O'Connor.)

last of the Mohicans—The last survivor(s). (From the book of the same name by James Fenimore Cooper.)

latch on to—To cling to; to get possession of.

Latter-day Saints—A Mormon body, founded in 1852, that regards itself as the successor of the church founded by Joseph Smith.

laugh on the other side of one's face—To change from amusement to dismay.

laugh up one's sleeve—To laugh secretly, while inwardly rejoicing or ridiculing someone. (In bygone days, a man could easily conceal a laugh in his large sleeves.)

laundry list—A long list, usu. of assorted items.

laying on of hands—The act of laying hands on a person's head in a religious ceremony.

lay it on thick—To flatter excessively.

lay it on with a trowel—To flatter or eulogize excessively. "Well said, that was laid on with a trowel"—from Shakespeare's *As You Like It*.

lay of the land—General state or condition of affairs under consideration; the facts of a situation.

lay siege to—To start besieging.

lead balloon—A flop; a joke or suggestion not well received.

lead down the garden path—See *garden path*.

leading edge—The forward part of something that moves or seems to move; an advantage.

lead-pipe cinch—Something very easy or certain.

lead someone a merry chase—To cause someone a lot of trouble.

leaf out of someone's book—See *take a leaf*.

leaps and bounds, by—Rapid progress.

left-handed compliment—One that is ambiguous in meaning or backhanded.

leg up—When you give someone a leg up, you help him overcome difficulties or obstacles.

le mot juste—See *mot juste*.

lese majeste—(F.) High treason.

let alone—To say nothing of. (He can't control his own children, let alone his stepsons.)

let sleeping dogs lie—Let well enough alone. "It is nought good a sleeping hound to wake," Chaucer's *Troilus and Criseyda*.

let the chips fall where they may—Never mind the consequences.

let them eat cake—Tactless remark attributed to Marie Antoinette on being told the people had no bread.

level with—To tell the truth.

lick and a promise—Perfunctory performance of a task.

lick into shape—To make workable or presentable.

lick one's chops (or **lips**)—To anticipate with delight.

lick one's wounds—To recuperate after a defeat.

lie in one's teeth—To lie blatantly.

lie low—To conceal oneself or one's intentions.

lie of the land—Same as *lay of the land* (more Brit. than U.S.)

life of Riley—A carefree way of living. Probably from a popular song of the 1890s. (Some authorities spell it Reilly, but Riley seems the more common.)

light-fingered—Adroit at stealing.

light-o'-love—Casual sweetheart; prostitute.

like a house afire (or **on fire**)—Fast; vigorously.

line of sight—Line from an observer's eye to a certain point; straight path between radio or TV transmitting and receiving antennas. (Sometimes erroneously written line of *site*.)

lingua franca—(It.) A common language spoken by people of different nationalities, usu. for commercial purposes.

lining one's pockets—Making money, usu. by unethical or illegal means.

lion's share—Usually considered the principal or largest part, though *Aesop's Fables,* from which it comes, makes it clear that the lion took the whole thing.

lip service, to pay—To state that one approves of something but fail to support it by action.

lip sync—Synchronizing movement of lips with recorded sound.

loaded for bear—Prepared for a major adversary.

loaded question—One that's worded unfairly.

loaded to the gills—Sometimes said of a person who drinks like a fish.

load the dice—To weight the dice, giving the owner an unfair advantage; to take unfair advantage of.

lo and behold—Used to express wonder or surprise.

lock, stock, and barrel—Entirely, completely. This phrase, which dates from about 1820, refers to a blunderbuss.

locus standi—(L.) Recognized position; standing in court.

loggerheads, at—Engaged in a quarrel. Since a loggerhead is a blockhead or stupid person, this is usually a stupid quarrel.

long and short of it—The gist of something.

long in the tooth—Getting on in years. From horse-trading.

look down one's nose at—To treat with contempt.

loss leader—A real bargain, offered to attract customers for other merchandise.

lower the boom—To crack down on; of nautical origin.

low-water mark—The level reached at low water; the lowest point or value.

luck of the draw—One's chances, good or bad.

luck out—To make a fortunate recovery; to come up smelling like a rose.

lynch law—Mob rule.

M

mad as a hatter; mad as a March hare—The former phrase predates *Alice in Wonderland*—the minds of hatters were often affected by mercury poisoning from a compound for making hats.

madding crowd—See *far from.*

made out of whole cloth—A complete fabrication. (Seldom heard except in lawyers' closing arguments.)

Mae West—An inflatable life jacket.

magna cum laude—(L.) With great praise.

magnum opus—(L.) A writer's or other artist's chief production.

maiden speech (voyage, etc.)—The first one.

maitre d'hotel (or **maitre d'**)—(F.) Headwaiter.

make mincemeat of—To demolish.

make no bones—To be straightforward, sure of. (Bones = dice.)

make, on the—See *on the make.*

make-or-break—(Adj.) Allowing no middle ground between success and failure.

make sport of—To ridicule.

make-work—Work assigned mostly to keep one busy.

malice aforethought—A predetermination to commit an act without legal justification or excuse.

malum in se—(L.) An offense that is wrong from its own nature, regardless of statute.

malum prohibitum—(L.) An offense prohibited by statute but not inherently wrong.

manner born, to the—Born to rank and wealth. Some authorities insist it should be to the *manor* born, but most cite Shakespeare's *Hamlet:* "But to my mind—though I am native here/And to the manner born—it is a custom/More honor'd in the breach than the observance."

many's the time—Often.

mare's nest—A hoax; a hopelessly snarled situation. From ca. 1619.

mark my words—Heed what I say.

Mary Jane—Marijuana.

mat, go to the—To engage in a hotly fought struggle (usu. verbal and ideological). Probably from wrestling.

McCoy (the real)—The genuine article, the real thing. Commonly associated with a boxer of the late 1890s known as Kid McCoy.

mea culpa—(L.) I am guilty.

meat-and-potatoes—(Adj.) Basic; everyday.

menage a trois—(F.) Lit., a household of three—usu. a married pair and the lover of one.

mensa et thoro—See *a mensa.*

mens rea—(L.) Lit., a guilty mind; criminal intent.

metes and bounds—The boundary lines of land, with their terminal points and angles.

method in his madness—See *there's a method.*

mettle, on one's—Aroused to do one's best.

Mickey Finn—A knockout drink, usu. one containing a drop or two of chloral hydrate. No one knows who the original Mickey was.

mickey mouse—(Adj.) Lacking importance; small-time.

Midas touch—The ability to make money in everything one undertakes.

midnight oil—Late hours.

might and main—With all one's strength and energy.

milk run—An expression originating among RAF pilots in Word War II to describe a regular sortie against an easy target—now refers to a routine, easy task.

mind-blowing—Overwhelming or astounding, affecting one in the manner of a psychedelic drug.

mind-boggling (or **it boggles one's mind**)—Overwhelming or astounding. To boggle is to frighten or alarm—the word probably comes from *bogle:* a goblin or scarecrow.

mind-set—Mental inclination, tendency, or habit; fixed state of mind.

mind's eye—The faculty of imagination.

mind your P's and Q's—Be careful. Probably from printing: a typesetter's problems with the two letters.

mirabile dictu—Wonderful to relate. (L., from Virgil.)

mise-en-scene—(F.) Stage setting; environment.

misery loves company—This goes all the way back to 1670: from John Ray's *British Proverbs.*

missionary position—A coital position with the female on her back, male on top with his face opposite hers. (Said to be the only coital position approved by missionaries.)

mixed bag—A motley assortment.

mock-up—A full-size structural model. (Some people pronounce *mark-up* almost the same.)

modus operandi—(L.) The mode of operation.

modus vivendi—(L., way of living) A feasible arrangement or practical compromise.

Molotov cocktail—A crude homemade bomb.

mom-and-pop—A small owner-operated business.

moment of truth—A moment of crisis; final sword thrust in bullfight.

monkey on one's back—A desperate desire for or addiction to drugs/alcohol.

monkey see, monkey do—Imitative behavior.

Montezuma's revenge—Diarrhea contracted by tourists in Mexico.

moot court—A mock court.

moot question—Debatable.

mopped up—Cleaned up (as in the stock market); destroyed remaining enemy resistance.

more honored in the breach than in the observance—Applied to a custom more generally neglected than observed. From *Hamlet.* See *manner born,* above.)

more's the pity—What a shame! Unfortunately.

mother lode—A rich vein of metal ore; an important source of supply.

mot juste—(F.) Exactly the right word or phrase.

motley crew—A varied assortment of people.

motor-mouth—One who talks constantly and rapidly. (This word has not yet made the dictionaries; when it does, it may or may not be hyphenated.)

Mr. Charlie—(Black Eng.) Disparaging term for a white man or white people.

Mrs. Grundy—One who displays prudish conventionality. (From Thomas Middleton's *Speed the Plough,* 1813.)

muck about (or **around**)—To mess around.

muddy the waters—To confuse the issue deliberately.

mumbo-jumbo—Gibberish; confused activity.

mum's the word—Sh!

murder will out—Chaucer wrote in about 1387, in *Canterbury Tales*, "Modre wol out, certeyn, it wol nat faille."

Murphy's Law—"If anything can go wrong, it will." Origin obscure.

muscle in—To force one's way in.

musical chairs—A game; a situation suggesting the game, because of rapid changes or confusing activity.

"Music has charms to soothe a savage breast"—From William Congreve's *Love for Love* (1695). It's frequently misquoted, such as: Music hath charms to soothe the savage beast.

N

namby-pamby—Sentimental, insipid, puny. Based on baby-talk. The original Amby (namby) was the poet Ambrose Phillips, born in 1671.

name of the game—The essential quality or matter.

narrow squeak—Close shave.

near miss—Something that narrowly falls short of its target or of success.

neck and neck—Very close, as in a race.

necktie party—A hanging, particularly by lynch law.

ne'er-do-well—An idle or worthless person.

neither fish nor flesh nor good red herring—Says Holt, "The notion is that of being nothing in particular—food neither for monks, for ordinary people, nor for paupers. The expression is Elizabethan."

neither fish nor fowl—Unclassifiable.

neither here nor there—Of no importance or relevance.

neither rhyme nor reason (sometimes **without rhyme or reason**)—Nonsense. "From that time unto this season,/ I received nor rhyme nor reason." Edmund Spenser, 1662.

ne plus ultra—(L.) The highest point capable of being attained; acme.

nerve-racking—Extremely trying on the nerves.

never-never land—An ideal or imaginary place.

next friend—One acting for the benefit of an infant or other person without being legally appointed guardian.

nice Nelly—A prude.

nickel-and-dime—(Adj.) Small-time. (Verb, without hyphens) To impair or weaken through small losses or niggling attention to details. (He nickeled and dimed us into bankruptcy.)

nickel bag—$5 worth of drugs.

nick of time—Critical moment.

nine days' wonder—A matter of intense but brief interest.

nines, dressed to the: See *dressed to the nines*.

nip and tuck—Closely contested; neck and neck.

nip in the bud—To destroy before something has had time to develop.

nitty-gritty—Essential, basic.

noblesse oblige—(F.) Obligations associated with high rank.

nodding acquaintance—Superficial acquaintance.

no great shakes—See *shakes*.

nolle prosequi—(L.) "I will no further prosecute."

nolo contendere—(L.) "I will not contest it."

nom de guerre—(F.) Lit., war name; pseudonym.

nom de plume—(F.) Pen name.

no-man's-land—An unoccupied area between opposing armies.

non compos mentis—(L.) Not of sound mind; insane.

no-see-um—A tiny stinging gnat; a punkie.

non sequitur—(L., lit. it does not follow) An inference that does not follow from the premise; a statement or response that does not follow logically from something previously said.

nota bene—(L.) Mark well; note this. (Abbrev.: n.b.)

not dry behind the ears—Inexperienced.

not kosher—Not proper.

not to put too fine a point upon it—To speak bluntly. (*Bleak House,* Dickens.)

not turn a hair—See *turn.*

not wisely but too well—From Shakespeare's *Othello:* "Of one that lov'd not wisely but too well."

nouveau riche—(F.) Newly rich.

numero uno—(S.) Number one.

nunc pro tunc—(L.) Now for then.

nuts and bolts—(Noun) The working parts or elements. (Adj., with hyphens) Nitty-gritty.

O

obiter dictum—An incidental remark, esp. by a judge.

objet d'art—(F.) An article of some artistic value.

odd as Dick's hatband—See *Dick's hatband.*

odd man out—One that is eccentric or unorthodox.

odor of sanctity—An appearance of or reputation for goodness and righteousness.

off one's rocker (trolley)—See *rocker, trolley.*

off-putting—Disagreeable, repellent.

off-the-cuff, on-the-cuff—See *cuff.*

off the deep end—See *go off the deep end.*

off-the-wall—(Adj.) Offbeat, far out. (He has an off-the-wall sense of humor.)

offtrack betting—Pari-mutuel betting conducted away from the racetrack.

of two minds—See *two minds.*

oil on troubled waters, to pour—To bring calm from tumult. This dates from the 7th century.

old army game—A swindle.

old fogy—One who is tiresomely conservative or old-fashioned. (A *fogy,* or *fogey,* used to be military slang for a small increment in pay for each enlistment served.)

old guard—The stalwarts of any party, movement, or organization.

olive branch, to hold out the—To make overtures for peace.

on-again, off-again—Existing briefly, then disappearing in an unpredictable way.

on all fours—A phrase used to express the idea that a case at bar is in all points similar to another.

once and for all—Finally; conclusively. Says Bergen Evans, "The 'and' in *once and for all* seems to have been added solely for rhetorical emphasis. The phrase used to be *once for all.*"

one-armed (or **one-arm**) **bandit**—Slot machine.

one fell swoop—A single deadly action (as a hawk would swoop on his prey). The word *fell* comes from the old French *felon,* meaning savage, cruel.

one-upmanship (or **one-upsmanship**)—The art or practice of keeping one step ahead of a friend or competitor.

on one's mettle—To be stirred or persuaded to do one's utmost.

on one's uppers—See *uppers.*

on the make—Seeking sexual, financial, or political favors.

on the QT—On the quiet, off the record. From an 1870 ballad.

on the qui vive—Alert, on the lookout. From *qui vive* (L.), a sentry's cry of "Who goes there?"

on the take—Being illegally paid for favors.

on the wane—Growing weaker; approaching the end.

on the wrong tack—To take a wrong line, to be on the wrong line of action or conduct. Nautical.

on the wrong track—Following the wrong line of inquiry. (Similar meaning to the phrase above.)

open-and-shut—Simple, obvious, straightforward; easily settled.

open-ended—(Adj.) Not rigorously fixed.

opening gambit—Calculated move or stratagem. (The phrase is redundant, since gambit, a chess term, means an opening move.)

open sesame—A seemingly unfailing means for gaining admittance or achieving success. From the *Arabian Nights* tale of "Ali Baba and the Forty Thieves."

order of magnitude—A range of magnitude extending from some value to 10 times its value.

ordinary borrow—See *borrow*.

O tempora, O mores!—(L.) O the times, 0 the manners!

other side of the coin—On the other hand.

Ouji [trademark] **board**—A device on which one seeks to obtain a spiritualistic message.

out-and-out—Complete.

out at the elbows—To be ragged or obviously poor; from ca. 1840.

out-Herod Herod, to—To exceed in violence or extravagance. (From Shakespeare's *Othello*.)

out of hand—(1) Without delay, hesitation, or preparation; (2) out of control.

out of kilter—See *kilter*.

out-of-pocket—(Adj.) Describing an expense that requires an actual cash outlay.

out of sorts—Irritable; in a bad mood.

out of sync—Not perfectly synchronized; not meshed well.

out of the frying pan into the fire—Clear of one difficulty only to fall into a greater one.

out of whack—See *whack*.

over the hill—(Adj.) Past one's prime.

over the transom—Offered without prior solicitation, esp. for publication. (*NSR* receives an occasional over-the-transom article.)

p

paddle one's own canoe—To be independent.

paeans of praise—Redundant, since *paean* means a song of joyful praise or exultation.

paint the lily—To exaggerate the beauty or virtues of; to try to improve on perfection. (From Shakespeare's *King John*—usually misquoted as *gild* the lily.)

pale, beyond the—Irrevocably unacceptable or unreasonable. (*Pale* was originally a fence erected to protect a town.)

pale(s) into insignificance—Become(s) insignificant, unimportant.

palm off, to—To pass off fraudulently. Its origin is probably in sleight of hand.

palmy days—Prosperous or happy days.

palsy-walsy—Intimate or appearing to be.

Pandora's box—A box that, when opened, let loose all kinds of misfortunes upon mankind. From Gr. mythology. In modern usage, a prolific source of troubles.

panic button—Something that sets off an immediate emergency response.

pan out—To turn out well; to succeed.

paper over—To gloss over or to explain away; to conceal.

paper tiger—One that appears to be powerful or dangerous but is inwardly weak or ineffectual.

Pap test (or **smear**)—A test for early detection of uterine cancer, devised by George N. Papanicolaou.

par excellence—(F.) Regarded as the highest of something; preeminence.

Parkinson's Law—Any of several satirical observations by English historian Northcote Parkinson, especially "Work expands to fill the time available for its completion."

25

parol evidence—Oral evidence.

part and parcel—An essential or integral portion; from ca. 1830.

party line—The set or approved policy of a political party or other entity.

pas de deux—(F.) A dance or figure for two performers; an intricate relationship or activity involving two parties or things.

passing belief—Incredible.

pass muster—To secure approval or acceptance.

past master—One who is an expert in his subject.

patience of Job—Preeminent forbearance or long-suffering. Eric Partridge says there is no such phrase in the Bible; the *Book of Job* does not contain the word *patience*.

patient Griselda—A model of patience and endurance. (Heroine of the last tale of Boccaccio's *Decameron*. She also appears in Chaucer's *Canterbury Tales*.)

patron saint—A guardian saint of any person, place, or activity.

pause, to give—See *give pause to*.

pay dirt—Ore or earth that is profitable to a miner; useful or remunerative object.

pay out (a rope)—To let out gradually by slackening.

pay the piper—To bear the consequences of a pleasurable indulgence. (Probably from *The Pied Piper of Hamelin*, a poem by Robert Browning.)

pay through the nose—Alfred H. Holt suggests that "the most plausible derivation of this somewhat gruesome figure for paying till it hurts . . . is perhaps that the Swedish poll-tax was once called a 'nose-tax'."

PDQ—Pretty damn quick.

peanut gallery—Rear section of a theater's balcony.

pearls before swine—See *cast pearls*.

pea soup (or **pea souper**)—A heavy fog.

peeping Tom—A voyeur; one who watches someone undressing, etc. (The original peeping Tom was a tailor in the story of Lady Godiva.)

peg away at—To stick to something persistently.

pendente lite—(L.) During the litigation.

pendulum, swing of the—The tendency of public opinion to shift after a time.

penny ante—(Noun) Poker played for small stakes. (Adj., hyphenated) Small-time.

penny-wise and pound-foolish—Prudent only when dealing in small sums.

per curiam—(L.) By the court.

perk test—Short for percolation test: a test to determine the suitability of soil for a septic sewage system.

per os—(L.) By mouth (used in prescriptions).

per se—(L.) By himself or itself; in itself.

persona grata—(L.) An acceptable person, especially a diplomat acceptable to a foreign government.

persona non grata—(L.) Unacceptable person.

petard, hoist on one's own—See *hoist*.

peter out—To exhaust; to give out.

Peter Principle—(From the book of the same name by Laurence J. Peter) A theory that in a hierarchy each employee tends to rise to the level of his incompetence.

phase in (out)—To bring gradually into (or out of) use.

Phi Beta Kappa—A person who wins high scholastic distinction and is elected to a national honor society of the same name.

Philadelphia lawyer—A lawyer who specializes in loopholes, one with great talent for exposing weaknesses of opposition witnesses.

pick-me-up—Something that stimulates or restores.

pidgin English — A simplified form of speech, as used for communication between groups speaking different languages. *Pidgin* is a corruption of *business.*

piece de resistance — (F.) The main dish; the most important or remarkable item.

piece of cake — Something easily done; a cinch.

pied-a-terre — (F.) A temporary or second lodging.

pied piper — (From the *Pied Piper of Hamelin,* a poem by Robert Browning) One who offers strong enticement; a leader who makes irresponsible promises.

pie in the sky — An unrealistic prospect of future happiness.

pig in a poke — See *buy a pig in a poke.*

pillar of the church (community) — A main or enthusiastic supporter.

pillar to post, from — Here and there, at random. From an old form of handball played against one wall of a courtyard. To be *driven from pillar to post* is to be forced to go from one bad situation to another, "roughly equivalent to modern *between a rock and a hard place,*" says Ciardi.

pincer movement — An attack in which forces converge on both sides of an enemy position.

Ping-Pong — Table tennis. (This is a trademark and should be capitalized.)

pink elephants — Hallucinations arising from heavy drinking or narcotics.

pink slip — A notice that one's employment is being terminated.

pins and needles, on — Nervous and jumpy.

pipe down — To stop talking or making noise.

pipe dream — An illusion. (Orig., fantasies brought on by smoking opium.)

piss and vinegar — Energy, vivaciousness, mischievousness. (An old and somewhat vulgar expression.)

pitched battle — An intensely fought battle.

plague on both your houses, a — Down with both sides. (Shakespeare said, "A plague o' both your houses!" in *Romeo and Juliet.*)

plain as the nose on your face — Obvious. Rabelais wrote in 1552, "Plain as a nose in a man's face."

plate tectonics — (Geology) Modern continental drift theory.

play havoc with — To create havoc in.

play possum — To pretend to be asleep or dead; to lie low.

pleased as Punch — Greatly delighted. From the Punch-and-Judy puppet shows.

plight one's troth — To say one's marriage vows or to be engaged to be married.

Plimsoll line (or **mark**) — An indication of the maximum depth to which a vessel may be loaded.

plug-ugly — A thug; rowdy or unpleasant character. (This term is said to have originated in Baltimore, Md.)

plumb, out of (or **off**) — Out of vertical or true.

plumb the depths — To try to get to the bottom of.

plus ca change, plus c'est la meme chose — (F.) The more it changes, the more it is the same.

pocket veto — An indirect veto, when a president or governor holds a bill unsigned after adjournment of the legislature.

politics makes strange bedfellows — So said Charles Dudley Warner in 1870, in *My Summer in a Garden.* (Shakespeare, in *The Tempest,* wrote "Misery acquaints a man with strange bedfellows.")

pomp and circumstance — Ceremony.

Pooh Bah — A person who holds many offices at once. From *The Mikado,* by Gilbert and Sullivan.

poor mouth — A protestation of poverty. "When you ask him for a donation, he makes a poor mouth." Webster's Third.

27

poor thing, but mine own—A misquotation from Shakespeare's *As You Like It*, "An ill-favored thing, sir, but mine own."

pork barrel—Government funds used for political patronage, etc.

portal-to-portal—(Adj.) Relating to time spent by a worker in traveling between his home and place of employment.

portmanteau word—An invented word that combines the sounds and meanings of two words, such as *motel*.

port of call—A place where a ship stops during its journey.

powers that be—The people in authority.

precept and example—Rule and example. (A worn-out cliché.)

precious few (precious little)—Extremely few (little).

press (the) flesh—To shake hands.

pretty kettle of fish—See *kettle of fish*.

pretty penny—High cost.

preventive maintenance—Good care of equipment, etc., to forestall emergency measures. (Avoid *preventative*.)

prey on one's mind—To worry extremely. From ca. 1800.

prick up one's ears—To become suddenly attentive to.

pride of place—The most prominent position; awareness of one's position, amounting to arrogance.

prima donna—(It., literally first lady) The principal female singer in an opera, etc. Now wildely used to describe a person of either sex who is overly sensitive, vain, or undisciplined.

prime mover—Initial source of motive power.

primrose path—A way of life of worldly ease or pleasure. "Himself the primrose path of dalliance treads." Shakespeare's *Hamlet*.

pro bono publico—(L.) For the public good.

pro-choice—(Adj.) In favor of legal abortion.

Procrustean bed—An arbitrary standard to which exact conformance is enforced. Procrustes was a giant of Greek fable who shortened or stretched victims to fit an iron bed.

pro forma—A matter of form; perfunctory.

pro-life—(Adj.) Opposed to legalized abortion.

proof of the pudding is in the eating—You can't tell until you've tried it. From *Don Quixote*, by Cervantes.

prophet without honor (in his own country)—A cliché adapted from *Matthew 13:57*, "A prophet is not without honor, save in his own country, and in his own house."

propria persona—See *in propria persona*.

pros and cons—Arguments for and against. (Oddly, we sometimes see this spelled as *prose and cons*.)

pro tanto—(L.) As far as it goes; for what it's worth.

pro tempore—(L.) For the time being. *Pro tem.* is the contraction.

P's and Q's—See *mind your P's and Q's*.

psych oneself up—To prepare oneself emotionally.

pull a fast one—To perpetuate a fraud or trick.

pull the chestnuts out of the fire—To do someone else's illicit or dangerous work. From the fable of the monkey that used the cat's paw to pull chestnuts out of the fire—which is also the source of the term *cat's paw*, meaning a dupe, one used by another to accomplish one's own purpose.

pump iron—To lift weights.

pump priming—Stimulating the economy by public spending.

Punch-and-Judy show—A traditional puppet show.

punch-drunk—Dazed; confused.

push comes to shove, if—See *if push comes to shove*.

pussyfoot around—To move warily; to refrain from committing oneself.

put a bug in one's ear—To plant an idea.

put out to pasture—Retired, usu. against one's will.

puts and calls—(Stock market) A "put" is an option to sell a specified amount of a security or commodity within a fixed period of time; a "call" is an option to buy a security or commodity within a certain time.

put the kibosh on—To put an end to; dispose of. (The origin of the word *kibosh* is uncertain, though one theory is that is comes from *cie bais* [Irish], the last word being pronounced bosh, which means cap of death.)

put-up job—Something arranged fraudulently or secretly beforehand.

put up or shut up—Produce or keep quiet.

Pyrrhic victory—A victory as disastrous to the victors as to the vanquished. (King Pyrrhus, victorious at Asculum, 269 B.C.)

Q

quake in one's boots—To shake with terror, literally or figuratively.

quantum jump (or **leap**)—An abrupt transition or change; dramatic increase or advance.

quantum meruit—(L., lit. as much as he deserved) A count in a legal action based on the promise that the defendant would pay the plaintiff as much as the plaintiff deserved for his work.

quarter, give no—See *give no quarter*.

queer as Dick's hatband—See *Dick's hatband*.

quelque chose—(F.) Something.

qu'est-ce que c'est que ca?—(F.) What is that?

que sera sera—(S.) What will be will be.

queue up—To line up.

quid pro quo—(L.) Something given or received for something else.

quien sabe?—(S.) Who knows?

qui vive, on the—See *on the qui vive*.

quote, unquote—A device used by some people (particularly lawyers) to show that what they've just said, or are about to say, is a quotation.

quoth the raven ("Nevermore")—From Edgar Allen Poe's *The Raven*.

quo warranto—(L.) Lit., by what warrant? A proceeding seeking to prevent continued exercise of authority unlawfully asserted.

R

rabbit punch—A short chop with the edge of one's hand to the back of someone's neck.

rabble-rouser—One that stirs up masses of people.

rack and ruin, esp., **to go to r. and r.**—To fall into ruinous disrepair or neglect. From ca. 1599.

rack one's brains—To think hard about a problem.
rack up—To score; to accumulate. (He racked up 30 points.)
ragtag and bobtail—Rabble.
raise Cain—To make an uproar.
raison d'etre—(F.) Reason or justification for existence.
R & D—Research and development.
rank and file—Those people making up the body of an organization as distinguished from its leaders.
rant and rave—to carry on excessively.
rap on the knuckles—A reprimand; slap on the wrist.
rara avis—(L.) Lit., rare bird; wonderful thing.
rat on—To squeal on; to betray.
read-only memory—A computer memory that cannot be changed by the computer and that contains a special-purpose program.
read the riot act—To declare that a certain course of action must cease. The Riot Act was made law in England ca. 1720.
real McCoy—See *McCoy*.
real time—(Noun) The actual time during which something takes place. (Hyphenate when used as an adj.)
reckon with—To take into account.
red herring—Something that draws attention from the matter or issue at hand. From the use of red herring to distract hunting dogs from the scent.
reductio ad absurdum—(L.) Reduction to the absurd.
res gestae—(L.) Things done; transaction.
res ipsa loquitur—(L.) The thing speaks for itself. [Note: this phrase is here included because reporters sometimes misspell *loquitur.*]
res judicata—(L.) An adjudicated precedent in law. (Sometimes corrupted by lawyers to res *adjudicata*.)
rest on (upon) one's laurels—To be content with one's success. From an athletic victor's prize laurels.
rev up—To increase the speed of.

rhyme nor reason—See *neither rhyme nor reason.*
ride for a fall—To court disaster.
ride herd on—To keep a check on; to keep control over.
ride roughshod over—To treat inconsiderately.
rigged jury—Fixed jury.
rinky-dink—Old-fashioned; small-time.
ripple effect—A set of related consequences started by one event.
risk, at—At hazard; in danger.
rite of passage—A ritual used when a person reaches a new status in life, as adolescence, marriage, etc.
Robin Hood's barn—To be led all around Robin Hood's barn is to go on a fool's chase all around a thing but never to reach it. Now more commonly refers to the long way around.
rob Peter to pay Paul—To take from one person in order to pay another. From ca. 1400; origin dubious.
rocker, off one's—Not quite all there.
role model—A person whose behavior serves as a model for others.
role reversal—A change in customary functions (as a daughter who assumes her mother's normal responsibilities and privileges).
roll with the punches—To accept stoically whatever hard knocks life hands out. (From boxing.)
roman a clef—(F.) A novel in which real people and events are disguised as fiction.
rose by any other name—The full quote, from Shakespeare's *Romeo and Juliet:* "What's in a name? That which we call a rose/By any other name would smell as sweet."
rose-colored glasses—Optimistic eyes.
"Rose is a rose is a rose is a rose."—That's what Gertrude Stein wrote, *not* "*A* rose is a rose."
Rosh Hashanah—The Hebrew New Year.
round robin—A tournament in which each contestant is matched against every other contestant. The *robin* comes from the French *ruban* (ribbon).

rub a person's nose in it—To remind someone forcefully of an unpleasant fact.

Rube Goldberg—Describing a needlessly complicated gadget. Rube Goldberg was an American cartoonist (1883-1970) known for drawing comic drawings of ridiculously complicated "inventions."

Rubicon, cross the—See *cross*.

rule of thumb—See *by rule of thumb*.

run amok—See *amok*.

run foul (or afoul) of—To come into conflict with.

run riot—To behave in an unruly way.

run the gamut—To cover the whole range or course of.

run the gauntlet (or gantlet)—To face an ordeal in which gunfire, blows, criticism, etc., come from all sides.

rus in urbe—(L.) Lit., country in town; a place or house that combines country and city.

Russian roulette—A deadly game that consists of spinning the cylinder of a revolver loaded with one cartridge, then pointing the muzzle at one's own (or someone else's) head and pulling the trigger. By extension applied to any very dangerous activity.

S

sacred cow—An idea or institution that its advocates won't allow to be criticized.

sad sack—An inept person, esp. a soldier.

salad days (in one's)—In one's youth, inexperienced and very green. "My salad days,/When I was green in judgment." *Antony and Cleopatra*, Shakespeare.

salt away—To save (money).

salve one's conscience—To soothe one's conscience.

Sam Browne belt—A leather belt with a strap over the shoulder.

sanctum sanctorum—(L., holy of holies) An inviolably private place.

sans serif—Type without serifs. (The small lines finishing off the letter T, for example, are serifs.)

Santa Ana—A warm dry wind.

satchel-mouth—(Black Eng.) Person with a big mouth.

Saturday night special—A cheap handgun.

sauce for the goose—See *what's sauce*.

savoir faire—(F.) Polished social behavior; tact.

scarce as hen's teeth—Pretty scarce, since hens have no teeth.

scintilla of evidence—The slightest particle or trace of evidence. (*Scintilla*, L., means spark; *scintillating* comes from the same root.)

scorched-earth policy—The deliberate burning of crops, etc., that might be of use to an enemy occupying a country.

scot-free—Without payment or penalty of any sort. The "scot" has nothing to do with Scotland; in Middle English it was a tax.

scratch: from scratch, up to scratch—See *from scratch, up to scratch*.

screw up one's courage (screw one's courage to the sticking point)—To intensify one's courage to achieve a particular purpose. "Screw your courage to the sticking place,/And we'll not fail." *Macbeth*, Shakespeare.

scut work—Routine or often menial labor.

sea change, esp. to suffer a sea change—To be miraculously and much changed for the better. *The Tempest*, Shakespeare.

sea legs—Ability to walk on a rolling ship without seasickness.

seat-of-the-pants—(Adj.) Using personal experience or judgment rather than technical aids. (Not hyphenated in usage such as "He flies by the seat of his pants.")

second nature—A habit or characteristic that has become automatic.

security blanket—Something that gives one a sense of security.

31

seeded players—Players in a tennis tournament, e.g., expected to reach the final stages and who are so placed that they do not meet each other until the final rounds.

seized of—Possessed of.

seize up—A moving part is said to seize up when it ceases to function because of overheating or lack of lubrication.

sell down the river—To betray or defraud.

sell short—To sell a borrowed stock in the hopes of replacing it at a lower price.

set on one's ear—To put down; to give one his comeuppance.

set one's sights (on)—To aim for. (From surveying.)

set one's teeth on edge—To cause an unpleasant sensation.

set store by—To consider valuable, trustworthy, or worthwhile.

set-to—A usu. brief but vigorous contest. (Plural: set-tos.)

shake in one's shoes—To quake in one's boots; to be in a state of nervous terror.

shakes, no great—Of small importance or merit.

shake the dust from one's feet—To leave a place without intention of returning.

shanks' mare—One's own legs. To ride shanks' mare is to walk.

shelf, laid on (or **put on**)—Put aside as of no further use.

shell game—(From a game played with three walnut shells) A fraud; a swindle in which something of no value is substituted for a valuable item.

shilly-shally—To vacillate; hesitate. (This term dates from 1700.)

shoot from the hip—To act or speak hastily, without considering the consequences.

shooting gallery—A covered range for target practice; a place where one can obtain narcotics and shoot up.

shoot one's mouth off—To talk too freely.

shoot the breeze—To talk idly; to gossip.

shoot-the-chutes—An amusement-park ride.

short shrift—Curt treatment. In former times, a prisoner sentenced to death was allowed *shrift* (confession to a priest); often his executioners were impatient and allowed him only a short shrift.

shot wide (of) the mark—Was altogether in error (from target shooting).

show the white feather—See *white feather*.

shudder to think—To be appalled at the very thought of.

sic 'im/sic 'em—Says John Ciardi: "Verb forms are *sic, sicced, siccing* and also *sick, sicked, sicking*. Command used in setting a dog or dogs on a person, persons, or animal. Now means 'attack,' but in the earlier form *seek him, seek them,* the command to a dog to trail a scent."

sic transit gloria mundi—(L.) Thus passes away the glory of the world.

silk purse out of a sow's ear—See *you can't make.*

simon-pure—Real, genuine. The original Simon Pure was a character in a 1718 comedy, *A Bold Stroke for a Wife,* by Susan Centlivre.

sine die—(L.) Without (an assigned) day.

sine qua non—(L., without which [thing], nothing) An indispensable condition or thing.

siren song—An alluring or enticing utterance or appeal.

sixes and sevens, at—In a state of confusion or disorder. ("And everything is left at six and seven," Shakespeare, in *Richard II,* 1595; "Let things go at sixes and sevens," Cervantes, in *Don Quixote,* 1605; "But manly sette the world on six and seven," Chaucer, in *Troilus and Criseyde,* 1625; "Say, why is everything/ Either at sixes or at sevens?" W. S. Gilbert, in *H.M.S. Pinafore,* 1878.)

six of one and half a dozen of the other—No real difference.

sixth sense—Keen inductive power.
skin game—A swindling game or trick.
skin of my teeth—A hair's breadth; a narrow escape. *Job 19:20:* "My bone cleaveth to my skin and to my flesh, and I am escaped with the skin of my teeth."
slam dunk—Dunk shot, a shot in basketball made by jumping high into the air and slamming the ball down through the basket.
slap five—(Black Eng.) To slap another's palm in greeting.
slap on the wrist—A mild reprimand.
sleight of hand—Tricks or feats performed by magicians; legerdemain.
slush fund—A fund for bribing public officials, etc.
smart aleck—A know-it-all.
smart money—Money ventured by one having inside information or experience.
soft soap—(Noun) Flattery. (The verb form should be hyphenated: Don't try to soft-soap me.)
soft touch—One easily imposed on or taken advantage of.
son of a bitch—Bastard. *(Webster's Ninth New Collegiate Dictionary* does not hyphenate.)
sotto voce—(It., lit. "under voice") In an undertone.
sow one's wild oats—To be dissipated (and wild) when one is young and to reform afterwards.
sow's ear—See *you can't make.*
sow the wind and reap the whirlwind—To cause trouble and end up getting more than one bargained for. *Hosea 8:7:* "For they have sown the wind, and they shall reap the whirlwind."
spick-and-span—Fresh; brand new; spotlessly clean.
spill the beans—To give away a secret; to let the cat out of the bag.
spit and image (or **spitting image**)—An exact likeness. Ciardi says the term comes from ancient practices of black magic.
spit and polish—(Noun) Extreme attention to cleanliness and order.

split hairs—To make small, unimportant distinctions of meaning.
spread eagle—With outstretched arms and legs. (In bygone days, a man could be spread-eagled by being lashed to a ship's rigging and then flogged.)
spread like wildfire—To spread very fast.
square off—To assume a fighting stance.
square one (back to)—Back to the starting point of an enterprise, etc., with no progress made. From board games.
square the circle—To attempt the impossible.
stamping ground—Usual haunt of a person or animal.
stand pat—To stick firmly to what one has said.
stand treat—To pick up the check.
stare decisis—(L.) To abide by, or adhere to, decided cases.
state of the art—The current state of development or knowledge of a subject.
status quo—(L.) The existing state of affairs.
stave off—To fend off or ward off (e.g., to stave off criticism or starvation).
steal a march on—To gain an advantage over, unobserved.
steal one's thunder—To grab attention from another or to adopt someone's methods as one's own. *Brewer's Dictionary of Fact and Fable* says the phrase comes from the anecdote of John Dennis (1657-1734), who invented a device to produce stage thunder for his play. The play was a failure. Later Dennis, hearing his thunder used in *Macbeth,* exclaimed, "My God, the villains will play my thunder but not my plays!"
stew in one's own juice—To be obliged to suffer the consequences of one's own actions. (Earlier *stew in one's own grease.)*
sticking point—An item, as in a negotiation, likely to result in an impasse. (See also *screw up one's courage.)*
stick in one's craw (or **gizzard**)—To be unacceptable or offensive, something that one can't swallow.

stick-in-the-mud—Old fogy. (This dates from 1733.)

stick-to-itiveness—Tenacity.

stick to one's guns—To maintain one's position in the face of opposition.

stick to one's last—To stay with the work for which one is best fitted. ("Cobbler, stick to your last," common translation of a proverb from Pliny the Elder in third century B.C.)

stiff-necked—Haughty; stubborn.

still and all—Nevertheless.

stock-in-trade—The equipment necessary for a trade or profession.

stone-cold—Absolutely, completely. (This dates from 1592.)

storm in a teacup—Much ado about nothing.

stormy petrel—One fond of strife; harbinger of trouble.

straight and narrow—The way of propriety.

straight from the shoulder—With full force (from boxing).

straitened circumstances, in—Hard up.

straw in the wind—A small indication of how things may develop.

stream of consciousness—A style of writing containing a continuous flow of a person's thoughts.

strung out—(Black Eng.) In love or deeply infatuated; addicted to drugs.

Sturm und Drang—(G.) Turmoil.

subornation of perjury—The offense of procuring another to take such a false oath as would constitute perjury in the principal.

sub rosa—(L., under the rose) In confidence, in secrecy. The rose was an emblem of silence.

sudden infant death syndrome—Crib death. (Abbrev. SIDS.)

suffer fools gladly, (not) to—(Not) to be patient with the stupid and the foolish. *2 Corinthians 11:19:* "For ye suffer fools gladly, seeing ye yourselves are wise."

sufficient unto the day is the evil thereof—*Matthew 6:34.* Let's not borrow trouble. (The sentence that precedes it: "Take therefore no thought for the morrow: for the morrow shall take thought for the things of itself.") We understand this is a favorite phrase of a New York judge—who is sometimes surprised at the way it appears in the record.

sui generis—(L.) Of its own kind, unique; in a class by itself.

sui juris—(L.) Of one's own right; not under any legal disability or power of another.

summa cum laude—(L.) With highest praise or distinction.

swan song—Last work of a poet, composer, etc.

swear like a trooper—To swear forcibly.

sweetheart contract (or **agreement**)—An agreement between an employer and an employee on terms favorable to the employer, without approval of union membership.

sweet-talk—(Verb) To flatter.

swing of the pendulum—See *pendulum.*

swing shift—The work shift between the day and night shifts.

sword of Damocles—An impending disaster. (In classical mythology, the tyrant Dionysis gave a banquet, and, in order to show the precariousness of rank and power, had a sword hung above the head of Damocles suspended by a single hair—which wasn't much fun for poor Damocles.)

swords' points, at—Mutually antagonistic.

T

tabula rasa—(L., lit. smoothed or erased tablet) A mind entirely blank, before receiving outside impressions; something in its original pristine state.

tail off (or **away**)—To dwindle. (See *trail off*.)
take a bath—To suffer large financial losses.
take a gander—To look or glance at. Probably from a person's stretching his neck (like a gander) to look.
take a leaf out of someone's book—To follow someone's example.
take a powder—To leave hurriedly.
take down a peg—To take the conceit out of a person.
take it in (one's) stride—To do something without needing a special effort; to accept hardships or setbacks without complaint.
take it lying down—To accept without protest.
take it on the chin—To suffer a blow.
take it on the lam—To flee, esp. from the police.
take one's licks—To accept one's misfortune or punishment.
take, on the—See *on the take*.
take to task—To call to account for a shortcoming.
take umbrage—See *umbrage*.
take up the cudgels—To defend vigorously. (A cudgel is a short heavy club.)
takes two to tango (or **tangle**), **it**—One person alone can't be blamed for the situation
talk through one's hat—To talk with insufficient knowledge of one's subject.
talk out of both sides of one's mouth—To express opposing views, etc., depending on one's audience.
talk turkey—Talk business. William and Mary Morris suggest a charming origin to the term: A white man and a friendly Indian hunting together agreed to divide equally what they bagged. Having two turkeys and three crows at day's end, the white man took the turkeys and gave the crows to the Indian, who then complained, "You talk all turkey for you. Only talk crow for Indian."
tall order—Difficult task.
tant mieux—(F.) So much the better.
tant pis—(F.) So much the worse.

tar and feather—To punish someone by smearing with tar and then covering with feathers.
tarred with the same brush—To have the same faults as someone else. This may come from the tarring (marking) of sheep.
taut ship/tight ship—A taut ship is one whose crew is well disciplined and whose efficiency rating is high. Though *taut* is preferred to *tight* here, either is acceptable.
teed off—Angry.
teeming with—Abounding in; rich in.
telegraph one's punches—To reveal prematurely one's plans.
telling tales out of school—Tattling; revealing privileged information.
tempest in a teapot (or **teacup**)—Much ado about nothing.
tempus fugit—(L.) Time flies.
tenants by the entireties—A tenancy in which husband and wife are seized of the whole but without power of severing (in contrast to joint tenancy).
tenterhooks, on—To be in a state of painful suspense. Tenterhooks were hooks from which cloth was suspended, but the term was also applied to the hooks from which meat was hung in front of butcher shops. Bergen Evans thought it likely that "it was from this ghastly but common spectacle that this term arose." (There was nothing *tender* about such hooks, so be sure to spell the word right!)
terra firma—(L.) Dry land; solid ground.
terrible-tempered Mr. Bang—The original Mr. B. was a character in Fontaine Fox's cartoon strip "Toonerville Trolley" who was forever blowing his stack.
tete-a-tete—(F., lit. head to head) Private interview or conversation between two people.
tether, end of one's—Limit of one's endurance. (The reference is to an animal that can graze only as far as its tether [rope] will allow.)

there's a method in his madness—It's not entirely illogical. "Though this be madness, yet there is method in 't." Shakespeare's *Hamlet*.

third degree—Exhaustive questioning, or worse, by authorities in an attempt to get information or a confession. (From the Third Degree of the Masonic lodge. In order to achieve it, the candidate undergoes intensive questioning.)

thorn in one's flesh (or **side**)—A constant source of irritation.

three sheets in the wind.—(From sailing.) Dickens wrote in *Dombey and Son*, ". . . he was three sheets in the wind, or, in plain words, drunk."

throes of, in the—Struggling with the task of.

throw down the gauntlet (or **glove**)—To challenge to combat. From dueling.

throw in one's hand—To give up. From card playing.

throw in the sponge (or **towel**)—To admit defeat. From boxing.

throw out the baby with the bathwater—To destroy one's own project through an excess of zeal. (It's hard to remember that this tired saying was once fresh and funny.)

throw the book at—To make all possible charges against a person or to assess the maximum penalty.

ticky-tacky—Of a monotonous sameness; tacky.

tilt at windmills—To attack imaginary foes or abuses. From *Don Quixote*, Cervantes.

time and tide wait for no man—It's folly to procrastinate. (An old Scotch proverb.)

time-honored—Honored because of age or long tradition.

time immemorial—Time whereof the memory of man is not to the contrary. English law defines it as any time before the beginning of "legal memory" in 1189, the first year of the reign of Richard I.

time out of mind (or **memory**)—Time immemorial.

time's awasting—Tempus fugit. [Note—awasting is one word; no hyphen.]

time warp—An anomaly, discontinuity, or suspension occurring in the progress of time.

tinker's dam, not worth a—Worthless. A dam of mud, clay, etc., held solder in place as a tinker repaired a pot; it was then brushed away as of no further use. But several authorities, such as Bergen Evans, say it should be tinker's *damn*, a tinker's curse—and that spelling it *dam* is a mere avoidance of *damn*.

Tinker to Evers to Chance—Used to describe an effective progression or cooperative effort; sometimes it refers to passing the buck. (The three men, the "peerless trio" of the Chicago Cubs at the beginning of this century, were famous for their ability to make double plays.)

Tin Pan Alley—The world of composers and publishers of popular music.

tit for tat—Retaliation.

to boot—See *boot*.

toe the line (or **mark**)—To conform strickly to rules or standards.

tongue and groove—A joint made by a tongue of one edge of a board fitting into a groove of another board.

tongue in cheek—Speaking with insincerity or irony.

tongue-lashing—Scolding.

tooth and nail—With every available means.

top banana—A show's leading comedian; a person who excels or leads in his field.

top dog—The victor.

topsy-turvy—Upside down.

tote board—An electronically operated board at a racetrack.

tot up—To add up.

touch and go—A very narrow escape. Said of a ship that touched a reef, etc., while under way but was still able to sail on.

touch bottom—To reach the worst or lowest point.

tour de force—(F.) Outstanding performance or achievement.

tout de suite — (F.) Immediately.

trade-last — A compliment offered in exchange for another.

trail off — To leave incomplete, as a sentence. Same as *tail off*.

train of thought — The procession of (associated) thoughts through one's mind. Some people get the cliché wrong and say *trend of thought*.

travesty of justice — Mockery of justice.

treadmill, on a — Doing tiring, monotonous work.

tread on one's toes — To offend someone.

trial balloon — An experiment to see how the public will receive a planned policy or program.

trolley, off one's — Not quite all there.

trompe l'oeil — (F., lit. deceive the eye) Still-life deception; figuratively, illusion, sham, camouflage.

trooper, swear like a — See *swear*.

trot out — To produce. (He trotted out the same old lies.)

truck with (having no truck with) — If you refuse to have any truck with a man, you won't deal with him in any way. The *truck* comes from the French *troquer*, to barter.

trumped-up — Fraudulently concocted. (Trumped-up charges.)

tuckered out — Tired, exhausted.

tug-of-war — A contest in which two persons or teams pull on a rope; a struggle for supremacy between opponents or competitors.

tumble to — To grasp the meaning of something.

turf, one's own — One's own territory or neighborhood.

turn a hair, not — To show no agitation or have no scruples against.

turn the tables — To reverse conditions or relations.

turn turtle — To capsize, overturn.

'twas ever thus — Things don't change.

twiddle one's thumbs — To twist one thumb around the other; to do nothing.

twinkling of an eye — An instant.

twist one's arm — To coerce.

two-edged sword — Something that cuts both ways.

two minds, of — Undecided.

𝒰

ultra vires — (L., lit. beyond power) Beyond the scope or in excess of legal authority.

umbilical cord, cut the — To become independent of one's mother, etc.

umbrage, take — To take offense. *Umbrage* refers to shadow or shade. "It is a fine phrase," says Bergen Evans, "suggesting one shadowed in offended pride...."

unbosom oneself — To disclose one's thoughts or feelings; to get something off one's chest.

unclean hands — To come into court with unclean hands is to be not wholly free of the fault complained of.

Uncle Tom — A self-effacing or subservient black who is trying to make a favorable impression on whites.

under the aegis of — (Pronounced e'jis) Protected or sponsored by. From Greek mythology. (An aegis is a shield.)

under the gun — On the spot; subjected to severe grilling, etc.

under-the-table — (Adj.) Covert and usu. illegal. (Hyphenated only in the adjective form. Their dealings were strictly under the table.)

under the wire — At the finish line (e.g., in a horse race); right at the deadline or the last minute.

under way — In motion or in progress. [Note that this is two words, not one.] A vessel is said to be under way, not under *weigh*.

und so weiter — (G., last word pronounced vi'ter) And so forth.

unglued (or **unhinged**), **to come** — To become upset; to fall apart.

Universal Products Code—A barcode, printed on a supermarket package, to identify the product.
up-and-up, on the—Honest.
up a tree—In great difficulty.
up in arms—Angry; vigorously protesting.
upper crust—Highest social level.
uppers, on one's—In straitened circumstances.
upset price—The price below which something offered at auction may not be sold.
upset the applecart—To spoil someone's plans.
up the creek—In a difficult or unfortunate position. (Also *up the creek without a paddle*.)
up the wall—In a state of agitation, annoyance, or frustration. (His frequent carping letters drive me up the wall.)
up to scratch—Up to the accepted standard.
up to snuff—In normal health; up to standard.
up to the hilt—Completely, entirely. From a dagger thrust all the way in.

V

value-added tax—An incremental excise levied on the value of a product at each stage of its development or manufacture.
vanity press—A publishing house that publishes books at the author's expense.
velvet glove—Outward gentleness masking inflexibility. ("... an iron hand in a velvet glove.")
velvet, on or **in**—In a good financial position; in clover.
veni, vidi, vici—(L., I came, I saw, I conquered) Words attributed to Julius Caesar on announcing a major victory.

vicious circle—Applied esp. to an argument that goes full circle. Carlyle, 1843. (Also *vicious cycle*, but the authorities say that *vicious circle* is the proper idiom.)
vintage year—A year in which the wine is of top quality; a year of outstanding success.
vis-a-vis—(F., lit. face to face) Opposite; as compared to.
viva la difference!—(F.) Long live the difference! (Usu. used in reference to the difference between the sexes.)
voice-over—Unseen narrator in a movie or on TV.
vox populi—(L.) Voice of the people; public opinion.

W

waiting game—Withholding action awaiting a more favorable opportunity later.
wake of, in the—Close behind and in the same path of. (From the track left by a vessel in the water.)
wall, go to the—See *go to the wall*.
wall: off the wall, to the wall, up the wall—See *off the wall, to the wall, up the wall*.
walk a tightrope—To make one's way warily in a dangerous situation.
walking papers—Dismissal or discharge; pink slip.
wane, on the—See *on the wane*.
war chest—A fund earmarked for a war or campaign.
ward heeler—A worker for a political boss in a local area.
warm body—An unqualified person cynically placed in, or allowed to remain in, an often responsible job.
warm the cockles of one's heart—To make one rejoice or feel good.

warp and woof—Basis, foundation. (Warp: the threads running the long way, crossed by the woof, those threads running from selvedge to selvedge.)

warts and all—Without flattery, glossing over nothing.

wash dirty linen (or **laundry**) **in public**—To air publicly scandals or quarrels of one's family or organization.

wash, it will all come out in the—Everything will turn out all right in the end. (From the Spanish. It appears in Cervantes' *Don Quixote*.)

wash, it won't—You'll have to find something better than that. (Your story won't wash.)

wash one's hands of—To refuse responsibility for something.

water down—To dilute; to reduce the effectiveness of.

water down the drain—Something too late to mend; spilled milk.

water, first—See *first water*.

Waterloo, to meet one's—To be soundly defeated (as was Napoleon).

water off a duck's back, like—The comment, etc., doesn't sink in, leaves no impression. (Ducks have a special means of oiling their feathers to make them waterproof.)

water over the dam—Something beyond recall or reconsideration.

water under the bridge—When we say much water has flowed under the bridge since then, we mean much has happened in the meantime.

wave of the future—Seen as representing a trend that will inevitably prevail.

wax and wane—To increase, then decrease (as phases of the moon).

way of the future—Wave of the future.

weak sister—An ineffectual person or thing.

weasel words—Words used to remove any real force from the expression containing them.

weather eye open—See *keep a weather eye open*.

well-heeled—Wealthy. Brewer's Dictionary says "*Heeled* in Western U.S.A. means supplied with all necessities, particularly money and firearms."

well-nigh—Nearly; almost. (It was well-nigh impossible.)

Welsh rabbit—A cheese dish. [Note: *rabbit* is not a corruption of *rare-bit*, though many people fancy up the dish by calling it Welsh *rarebit*.]

wet behind the ears—Inexperienced. (Same as not dry behind the ears.)

wet nurse—A woman who suckles a child not her own.

wet one's whistle—To take a drink.

whack, out of—Inoperative.

what-d'you call it—Said of a thing whose name one can't remember.

what for—A reprimand; punishment. (He gave the young whippersnapper what for.)

what have you—Whatnot. (Apples, oranges, what have you.)

what's-his-name—Said of a person whose name one can't remember. (I'll never forget old what's-his-name.)

what's sauce for the goose is sauce for the gander—Reverse ERA, perhaps? Two can play at that game.

what-you-may-call-it—Thingamajig. (Sometimes spelled whatchamacallit.)

wheeler-dealer—A shrewd operator, in business or politics.

wheel is come full circle—Just retribution has followed. (The full line is, "The wheel is come to full circle," from Shakespeare's *King Lear*.) See also *come full circle*.

when the chips are down—When the time comes for a decision.

where ignorance is bliss—See *ignorance*.

whet one's appetite—To stimulate one's appetite (or interest).

while away—To pass (time) in a leisurely or interesting manner.

whip hand—The upper hand.

whistling Dixie, not just—(Most often heard as "You ain't just whistlin' Dixie.") Quite right.

white feather (to show the)—To show cowardice; a phrase from the cockpit.

white-hot—Fervid; zealous.

white paper—A report issued by a government or other body to give policy information.

whiz kid—A brilliant or successful young person.

whole cloth, made out of—See *made out of.*

whole-hog—(Adj.) Without reservation; completely. When used as a noun (go the whole hog) or as an adverb (accept the contract whole hog), it should not be hyphenated. See also *go whole hog.*

whole shebang—The whole thing.

whoop-de-do—Noisy activity.

whose ox is [being] gored (it makes a difference)—One's interests affect one's outlook. "It makes a difference whose ox is gored"—Martin Luther. Bartlett's *Familiar Quotations:* "This is the moral of the fable of the lawyer, the farmer, and the farmer's ox, which was included in NOAH WEBSTER, American Spelling Book [1802] entitled *The Partial Judge.*"

whys and wherefores—Reasons.

wide berth—See *give a wide berth.*

wide of the mark—Not even close.

widow-maker—A machine, etc., that endangers a workman.

wild and woolly—Not refined. (Note two l's in woolly.)

willy-nilly—Whether desired or not. From *will I nill I,* be I willing or unwilling.

will (or won't) wonders never cease—Imagine that!

window dressing—Displaying facts so as to create a good impression; outward appearance not substantiated by intrinsic worth.

wing it—To do something in an impromptu fashion or by guesswork.

win hands down—To win easily. Says Eric Partridge, "From a jockey's relaxing his hold on the reins and dropping his hands when victory is certain."

wink at—To overlook.

wit's end, at—At the end of one's mental resources.

without fear or favor—Impartially.

without rhyme or reason—See *neither rhyme nor reason.*

word of mouth—Oral communication. This phrase dates from 1553. (Hyphenate the adjective form.)

world-shaking—Earthshaking.

worm-eaten—Eaten by worms; moth-eaten; antiquated.

worm turns, the—The downtrodden one rebels. "The smallest worm will turn, being trodden on." Shakespeare's *King Henry VI, Part III.*

worst comes to worst, if: See *if worst.*

worst way, in the—Very much. [Note: this can often result in ambiguity, as in "He wanted to win in the worst way."]

worth one's salt—Worth one's salary. (*Salary* comes from L. *salarium,* salt money.)

wrack one's brains—See *rack one's brains.*

wreak havoc—To lay waste to. *Wreak* comes from the Anglo-Saxon *wrecan* and means to inflict or deliver a damaging blow. (It should not be confused with *wreck.*)

wreak vengeance on—To inflict great punishment on; to avenge.

X Y Z

y'all—You-all.

yea big (high, etc.**)**—So big (high). Mostly heard in the South; usu. accompanied by an indication of height, etc.

yellow-dog contract—A contract in which an employee agrees not to join a union.

yellow journalism (or press)—Sensational journalism.

BUSINESS REPLY MAIL
FIRST-CLASS MAIL   PERMIT NO 69155   LOS ANGELES, CA 90035

POSTAGE WILL BE PAID BY ADDRESSEE

Movieline
PO BOX 469004
ESCONDIDO CA 92046-9982

NO POSTAGE
NECESSARY
IF MAILED
IN THE
UNITED STATES

58% off Movieline newsstand price

12 issues only $15.00

☐ **Yes.** Send me 12 issues of Movieline at only $15.00. I save over $20.00!

Name _____

Address _____

City _____ State _____ Zip _____

☐ Bill me   ☐ Check enclosed

Please allow 4–6 weeks for delivery of first issue. Foreign (including Canada): surface mail 12 issues $36, payable in U.S. funds drawn on a U.S. bank.

Movieline

special issue
Hollywood style

Sharon Stone
"If I stopped laughing, I'd go insane"

Tinseltown's Ten Best-Dressed Actresses

Why do Sandra Bullock, Mel Gibson and Susan Sarandon dress this way

Fashion Disasters from Geena Davis to Alicia Silverstone

yeoman service (to do, perform) — To do efficient, useful work. *Yeoman* may be a contraction of *young man* (Middle English). "It did me yeoman's service." — *Hamlet.*

yin and yang — Chinese philosophy of passive (yin, female) and active (yang, male) cosmic forces.

you-all — All of you. A Southerner would usually say y'all and wouldn't use it as applying to one person (unless that person represented a family or group).

"You can't make a silk purse out of a sow's ear" — Quotation from Jonathan Swift's *Polite Conversation,* 1738. (But variations appeared a century or more earlier than that.)

APPENDIX

Our Native Idiom

As Goethe said, "Everyone hears only what he understands." Luckily, this isn't altogether true of people in our profession. We reporters have the most highly trained ears of anyone around; we're able, at least up to a point, to record sounds we *don't* understand, and hope to unscramble them later.

But the more we do understand, the more knowledge of words, idioms, accents, and so on we have at our command, the easier our jobs become—and the better our transcripts. And I feel that we sometimes overlook the importance of mastering our own idioms.

About 20 years ago, a young girl came to me seeking work as a transcriber. She was, she said, a fast typist, and had been an honor student in high school. I gave her a tape containing some slow dictation and left her alone with it. (Now I know that the best way of testing a potential transcriber—or potential court reporter, for that matter—is to administer a spelling test; but I didn't know that then.)

The two or three spelling errors I might have overlooked, but when I saw she had transcribed "be enlarge" (which made no sense) for "by and large," I knew she was hopeless. The girl didn't know her idioms.

I still remember a similar deficiency in my own idiomatic vocabulary when I was about 17. I was trying to read six short outlines in copperplate shorthand that made no sense to me. Much later I learned that the words were "the be-all and end-all." Though it's a fairly common expression—it comes from Shakespeare's *MacBeth*, which I hadn't read at that time—I'd never heard it before; it might as well have been Swahili.

If you'll examine bloopers in transcripts, or errors in test papers, you'll find a surprisingly large number of them can be laid at the door of the reporter's (or student's) unfamiliarity with idiomatic English.

Sometimes idiom misuse is a basic hearing problem. One of the bosses on the *Richmond Palladium-Item,* the Indiana newspaper I worked for (as a stenographer) right out of high school, was slightly hard of hearing. "It isn't worth a hell of a bean," she used to say. That's probably how she herself heard "hill of beans," a common idiom of that day. ("Hard of hearing" is an idiom now often replaced by "hearing-impaired.")

Did you ever stop to think why testimony of many a foreign-born witness is so difficult to report, even when speed and accent pose no real problem? It's because they aren't at home with our idioms. They don't use the prepositions, articles, and short adverbs we're used to. We normally not only write in phrases but *hear* in phrases. If the small words aren't what we expect, we must strain to hear every one, and it sometimes seems as though there's no context to it. For instance, the foreign-born witness may say "similar with" or "innocent from," and we're likely to find ourselves reporting what sound like strings of unrelated words.

Context: the reporter's greatest friend. *Webster's Collegiate* defines it as "the parts of a discourse that surround a word or passage and can throw light on its meaning." Often it's an idiomatic expression that will help throw light on that obscure passage.

Reporting just words, with no real

context, can be a jarring experience. One of the hardest assignments of my reporting career was a two-day deposition in which a witness read into the record terse entries in a longhand diary. The words were simple, and the witness wasn't fast; but there was absolutely no context to the entries. I almost went out of my mind.

Americans from various parts of the country also have their own idiom, of course, and reporting a witness from an unfamiliar region can hold surprises. For instance, among some people in Massachusetts you don't *have* a heart attack; you *take* one. Sometimes the common phrase "I don't think so" comes under attack: "If you don't think, you shouldn't speak. You mean 'I think not.' " This purist would be quite pained at "I don't guess," which is quite common in the South.

There's one current misuse of idiom that pains *me,* and that's "hone in on" instead of "home in on." The word "hone" has no other meaning than to sharpen, as a razor, or to whet. (Anyone who is confused on this word should visualize a homing pigeon, which homes in on its objective.)

What's the difference between an idiom and a cliché? Sometimes not much. The first two definitions of "idiom" in the *Collegiate* are "a. the language peculiar to a people or to a district, community, or class: DIALECT. b. the syntactical, grammatical, or structural form peculiar to a language." It defines "cliché" as "a trite phrase or expression."

We also, of course, have to contend with slang expressions, street talk (some of which you'll find in our glossary of Terms from the Drug Scene), jargon. It's hard to keep up with all this, since our language keeps changing. For instance, a *New Yorker* article says that "to pass on" is Hollywoodese for "say no to."

Clichés—we love 'em. True, we should avoid using them ourselves; but when we get a chance to write them in shorthand, they make our work easier. So the more of these trite phrases we're familiar with, the better off we are. In the idiom-cliché class we might put "His heart's in the right place," "My heart was in my mouth," "She has a heart of stone." But "to learn by heart" is a pure idiom—one we couldn't get along without. By the way, *Word and Phrase Origins,* by Alfred H. Holt, says that "to 'learn by heart' is exactly equivalent to the word *record* (Latin *cor,* heart or mind) and the French *se recorder.*"

Having hinted that we need more familiarity with our native idiom, what do I suggest doing about it? The best way to improve our knowledge of word usage is to acquire what Vermont Royster calls the reading addiction. (See his article in the April 1982 *NSR.*) I suspect if we analyzed our everyday idiom-cliché speech we'd find the Bible and Shakespeare as its two principal sources. (You remember the story of the girl who said she wouldn't waste her time reading Shakespeare, since it was nothing but a bunch of clichés.) But reading almost anything helps.

What, if anything, do our reporting schools do to help familiarize students with the almost limitless number of idioms in the English language?

There is a treasury of books on word origins that make fascinating reading. In my own library I have, among others, *Harper Dictionary of Contemporary Usage,* by William and Mary Morris ($15.95, Harper & Row); *Word Origins and Their Romantic Stories,* by Wilfred Funk ($6.95, Bell); *A Dictionary of Modern English Usage,* by H. W. Fowler ($12.50, Oxford—see Brooks on Books, January 1981 *NSR*). I've borrowed from a friend two paperbooks that I must buy for myself: *A Dictionary of Clichés,* by Eric Partridge ($1.35, Dutton), and the one mentioned above, *Phrase and Word Origins,* by Holt ($1.35, Dover Publications). I must also try to get *Slang and Its*

Analogues, by Farmer & Henley (Arno Press), and H. L. Mencken's *The American Langauge.* There are, of course, many others. Books of this type not only serve as reference works but, as I say, are fun to read.

Each language has its own idioms, but I wonder if English, which has borrowed from so many other languages, may not be one of the richest in idioms—and the most puzzling to someone trying to master it.

What do you understand when you hear someone say, "From there on it was all downhill"? It can mean, to use some other well-worn phrases, that the person (company, etc.), after an uphill fight, had won hands down, that it was now a piece of cake, as easy as pie, etc. Or it can mean that someone (or something) was over the hill, had hit the skids and was now half dead, not long for this world. First you have to know the context

—*M.L.G.*

BIBLIOGRAPHY

I. **Dictionaries** [listed in order of usefulness to the author rather than alphabetically]

Webster's Ninth New Collegiate Dictionary—Merriam-Webster Inc.
Oxford American Dictionary—Oxford University Press
Webster's Second New International Dictionary—Merriam-Webster Inc.
American Heritage Dictionary of the English Language—Houghton Mifflin Company
Webster's Third New International Dictionary—Merriam-Webster Inc.
Random House Dictionary of the English Language—Random House
Oxford English Dictionary—Oxford University Press
6,000 Words—Merriam-Webster Inc.
Black's Law Dictionary—West Publishing Company
Blakiston's New Gould Medical Dictionary—McGraw-Hill
Dictionary of Foreign Words and Phrases—Philosophical Library

II. **Other Reference Works** [listed alphabetically]

Bartlett's Familiar Quotations—Little, Brown
Brewer's Dictionary of Phrase and Fable—Harper & Row
Comfortable Words, by Bergen Evans—Random House
Dictionary of American Slang—Thomas Y. Crowell Company
Dictionary of Catch Phrases, by Eric Partridge—Stein and Day (Scarborough)
Dictionary of Clichés, by Eric Partridge—Dutton
Dictionary of Contemporary American Usage, by Bergen and Cornelia Evans—Random House
Dictionary of Quotations, by Bergan Evans—Delacorte Press
Dictionary of Word and Phrase Origins, by William and Mary Morris—Harper & Row
Harper's Dictionary of Contemporary Usage, by William and Mary Morris—Harper & Row
Modern American Usage, by Wilson Follett—Hill and Wang
Modern English Usage, by H. W. Fowler—Oxford University Press
Oxford Dictionary of Quotations—Oxford University Press
Phrase and Word Origins, by Alfred H. Holt—Dover
Slang and Its Analogues, by J. S. Farmer and W. E. Henley—Arno Press

NOTE: Some of the publishers listed are those of paperback editions and thus may not be a book's primary publisher.

Antoinette Jones